JESUS:

A Living Example of Worship

JESUS:

A Living Example of Worship

by

Judson

Cornwall

Bridge-Logos *Publishers*
North Brunswick, NJ

Jesus: A Living Example of Worship
Copyright © 1997 by Judson Cornwall
All rights reserved
Printed in The United States of America
Library of Congress Catalog Card Number: 97-73690
International Standard Book Number: 0-88270-742-6

Bridge-Logos *Publishers*
North Brunswick Corporate Center
1300 Airport Road, Suite E
North Brunswick, NJ 08902

Dedication

To Dan and Judy Little,
my son and daughter in the Lord.
A precious couple who have
embraced worship for their own lives
and home and have faithfully taught
it to the congregation they pastor.
They are more than instructors in worship;
they are worshipers.

Contents

Preface

When we look to the Bible for examples of worship, we usually look to holy men of God long dead. We view Abraham's willingness to offer Isaac on Mount Moriah as a great example of unselfish worship. Similarly we view the life of Moses and his dedication to the will of God as the quintessence of living a life of worship. Or, more likely, we go to David whose songs of worship have so inspired others to worship. These, and other men and women of the Old Testament, were worshipers of the one true God, and their examples are worth emulating, but they are dead.

Jesus is a far better example of worship than any of these. He is unparalleled as a worshiper. No one ever worshiped the Father as did Jesus. He has become heaven's perfect example of worship, and He is still alive. He told John on the isle of Patmos, "I am the Living One; I was dead, and behold I am alive for ever and ever! And I hold the keys of death and Hades" (Revelation 1:18).

We cannot overemphasize the importance of worship. It has been a personal delight to see it come to the forefront in the past decade with a proliferation of books, tapes, songs, videos, and conferences on worship. We've been told and shown how, why, and when to worship, but it may be possible that in our over-emphasis on the how of worship, we have reduced the Bible's concept of worship more than we enlarged it. One could easily leave most of our worship conferences with a conviction that worship is a musical presentation, punctuated with banners and dancing.

In all of our worship instructions has anyone addressed the question, "Did Jesus worship? If so whom, when, where, how?" Just because we have no written record of Jesus shouting, dancing, waving banners, or standing for long singing sessions does not establish that He was a non-worshiper.

It is highly probable that Jesus had a greater awareness than we do of the true object of worship. His relationship with His Father was so intimate and personal that He did not need to come outside of Himself to worship in spirit and in truth. We can learn more about higher realms of worship by taking another look at how Jesus worshiped.

Ten years ago, my book titled, *Worship As Jesus Taught It*, was released. It had a limited circulation and went through one small printing. Rather than releasing it again as it was, I have adjusted portions of it to fit this new theme. Truths taught in the former book make up about sixty percent of this book. The first portion of the book shows Jesus active in helping us to worship. The second portion is totally new and presents Jesus as a worshiper.

Although most Christians are comfortable with the truth that Jesus is a proper object of worship, few seem to realize that He, while here on earth, was a worshiper of the Father. His humanity needed to worship, as surely as ours does. Beyond this human need, His divine nature longed to touch the divine realms, and worship was the means He used to maintain an intimate relationship with His Father.

Perhaps we, who are natural persons and sons and daughters of God, can benefit by seeing the difference in worship responses between the outer nature and the inner nature where the Spirit of God resides. Jesus is a living example of the latter form of worship.

Judson Cornwall

1

Jesus Introduced

If God had waited until late in the twentieth century, the coming of Jesus could have been heralded with tremendous fanfare. A dramatic ad could have run on television during the Super Bowl, or a mass mailing could have gone out to all religious groups. Perhaps the Internet could have been used to announce the coming of Jesus, and e-mail could have almost instantly alerted millions of persons throughout the electronic world.

The Madison Avenue publicity men could certainly have informed the world that an event of unprecedented magnitude was coming. Radio could have blared it, television could have illustrated it, and magazines and newspapers could have written lead articles about it. Headlines might have read: GOD IS ABOUT TO BECOME MAN!

But God chose to send His Son into the world before these modern means of communication were available. As always, He seemed content to do it His way. God has never needed hype to precede His intervention into the affairs of mankind. What a shame that modern religion does not recognize this.

God slipped Jesus into this world in the most obscure, humble manner imaginable. He ignored the palace, sidestepped the great Roman government, and even bypassed the religious powers of the day, although each of these was to play a part later in the ministry of Jesus.

For God's purposes, a manger was as useful as a plush nursery, and a peasant girl as valuable as a queen. A carpenter would be good enough for a stepfather, and the journey into Egypt by donkey was as effective as a jet airplane. It is amazing how little of what we consider valuable is necessary in the program of God. He needs little of what we have, and if what He needs is unavailable, He can create it on the spot.

The miracle of Christ's coming into our world was never dependent upon our affluence, nor contingent upon people's faith. Paul put it so succinctly when he wrote, *"But when the time had fully come, God sent his Son, born of a woman, born under law, to redeem those under law, that we might receive the full rights of sons"* (Galatians 4:4-5). When God was ready, it happened. All that remained was to let a few persons know what was happening.

God's Light Came in a Dark Season

Just as a painter puts in a darker background to enhance the figures in the foreground, we may need to take a brief glance at the state of religion in Israel at the time of the birth of Jesus. It might also help to know a little about the main characters who play key roles in the invasion of Jesus into our time/space dimensional world.

It was a bleak and dismal period of time in Israel's history when Jesus invaded it. Their national glory had long ago dissipated. Jesus came during a 500-year season in which Israel had no anointed prophet, priest, or king. They were dark years of apostasy, departure from God, and eventual subjugation to the powerful rule of the iron fist of Rome. The religion of the Jews that had consistently formed the backbone of the nation was greatly weakened by the warring factions of the two principal schools of interpretation: the Pharisees, who were the fundamentalists of their day; and the Sadducees, who were the liberals. Add to these the splinter groups who espoused neither of these religious philosophies, and it's not difficult to realize how fragmented the religion of the Jews had become by the time of Jesus.

Perhaps the only unifying force left to the Jews was the Temple and the promised Messiah, but even that was weakened by the absence of an anointed Word from God, and by constant arguments over interpretations of the Law. Religion had ceased to be a blessing and had become a burden. The joy of worship had been replaced with endless rituals that affected every waking moment of the Jews. Those who prayed for the Messiah to come did so more out of desperation than out of faith.

Life under Roman rule was bad enough, but life under the control of the religious leaders was intolerable. Religion without the divine presence has always been odious and onerous. Particularly loathsome is a religion that has experienced the anointed ministry of a prophet like Isaiah, a priest like Zadok, or a king like David, and then is reduced to function amidst the tension of two opposing ideologies— neither of which has evidence of God's presence. Who needs dead dogma to cloud the skies of our religious life? The cry of man's spirit is for God, not for mere interpretations of God's principles.

This lack of true spiritual life, however, did not cause the people to abandon their religion; it merely made them feel that their religion had abandoned them. The rituals of the religious faith of the Jews continued as usual. Sacrifices were offered just as the Law prescribed, and the priesthood functioned in harmony with the ancient instructions of Moses to Aaron. It was "business as usual" even though God hadn't been heard from for over five hundred years.

Didn't the Jews expect a coming Messiah? After all, their great prophet Isaiah foretold:

> *For unto us a child is born, unto us a son is given: and the government shall be upon his shoulder: and his name shall be called Wonderful, Counsellor, The mighty God, The everlasting Father, The Prince of Peace.*
>
> *Of the increase of his government and peace there shall be no end, upon the throne of David, and upon his kingdom, to order it, and to establish it with judgment and with justice from henceforth even for ever. The zeal of the LORD of hosts will perform this.*
>
> (Isaiah 9:6-7, KJV)

The Jews knew the promise, but they didn't recognize the person who came as the fulfillment of that promise. Jesus came differently than they had supposed He would. Doesn't He always?

The final book of the Old Testament had promised, *"Behold, I will send you Elijah the prophet before the coming of the great and dreadful day of the LORD"* (Malachi 4:5, KJV). Jesus told them that John the Baptist was this promised "Elijah," but they didn't recognize him or receive him any more than they recognized and received the One of whom he

4

told. How we forget that God isn't what or who we think He is. God is Who He says He is.

Zacharias And Elizabeth Were Informed

It may have been in the month of June [about 6 B.C.], as an aging priest was faithfully doing what he had been chosen to do, when God interposed Himself into the affairs of religion. He sent Gabriel to inform this officiating priest that in spite of his advanced years, he and his elderly wife were going to have a son—the "Elijah the prophet" promised in Malachi—who would be the forerunner of the Messiah. The angel's exact words were: *"And he will turn many of the children of Israel to the Lord their God. He also will go before Him in the spirit and power of Elijah"* (Luke 1:16-17, NKJV).

As usual, God had made a good choice. Zacharias and Elizabeth *"were both righteous before God, walking in all the commandments and ordinances of the Lord blameless"* (Luke 1:6, NKJV). Zacharias did not abandon the priesthood because of the emptiness of religion in his day. He faithfully carried out the duties of his office as God had prescribed in the desire that, somehow, it would bless God and benefit man.

That he was a worshiper of God is obvious from the fact that when the angel appeared to him, he was burning incense before the Lord in the Holy Place—the highest form of worship that temple service offered. This may have been mere ritual to others, but no doubt it had become very real to this dedicated priest.

We dare not condemn Zacharias for arguing with Gabriel, for this sort of divine intervention into the rituals of religion had not happened for so long that no one expected it, and few even believed that it was possible. By this time the Sadducees openly denied the existence of angels altogether. It is always hard on our faith when God does things contrary to our

5

espoused doctrinal beliefs. Fortunately, however, the priest's faith was not a prerequisite for God's intervention, either there in the Holy Place or later in his bedroom. Our sovereign God is not limited by the beliefs of foolish men.

When his tour of duty was over, Zacharias found the two-day walk back to the priestly city of Hebron more lonely than ever, inasmuch as he had lost his power of speech. Perhaps this was ordained of God, not only as chastisement from his unbelief, but also to prevent him from talking away the excitement and glory of this visitation. Furthermore, it gave him many hours of solitude to try to develop a way of explaining this visitation and promise to his devoted wife, who, in all probability, had not been privileged with sufficient education to read and write. Sign language can prove to be insufficient for expressing deep emotion.

The method of communication this excited husband may have settled upon proved to be unimportant, for just as surely as Zacharias found himself mute, Elizabeth found herself pregnant because of the promise of Gabriel. The positive affirmation of Gabriel that "*you will have joy and gladness, and many will rejoice at his birth*" (Luke 1:14, NKJV), began for this godly couple as soon as the pregnancy was confirmed. They did not need to hold the baby in their arms to be full of joy. Zacharias had the word of Gabriel, and Elizabeth had the baby in her womb. They could rejoice in the beginning of this miracle, while others would have to await the consummation of God's Word at the birth of John the Baptist.

Mary Is Chosen

About six months later, Gabriel appeared to the teenage girl in the rural village of Nazareth far from the Temple in Jerusalem, and several days' journey from Hebron—and introduced his presence with the salutation: "*Rejoice, highly favored one, the Lord is with you; blessed are you among women!*" (Luke 1:28, NKJV). This startling announcement was followed with even more unbelievable news as he told Mary: "*You will conceive in your womb and bring forth a Son, and shall call His name JESUS. He will be great, and will be called the Son of the Highest*" (Luke 1:31-32, NKJV).

How much of this Mary understood is often questioned, but when God speaks to the human spirit, there is a flow of faith that transcends the comprehension of the mind. Although she was but a village girl, she seemed to be well-steeped in Messianic hope and prophecies. She had heard the angel say that not only were these hopes going to be fulfilled, but that they were going to be fulfilled through her.

This meant that Gabriel was asking her to submit to a pregnancy before she was married. That would certainly cost her the future husband in her life—Joseph. It would forever destroy her reputation as a chaste virgin, and it might very well mean the loss of her life, for the provision of the Law for premarital pregnancy was death by stoning.

The stakes were high: great honor, but great disgrace. It was a chance to bless the world with a Savior that held an equal risk of being stoned to death before the Christ-Child was born. Crowns of greatness are generally preceded by crosses of suffering, but could such a young girl understand this?

When Gabriel told Mary that her cousin Elizabeth was already six months pregnant and added, "*For with God nothing will be impossible*" (Luke 1:37, NKJV), it settled Mary's mind. "*Then Mary said, 'Behold the maidservant of the Lord! Let it be to me according to your word'*" (Luke 1:38, NKJV). *Phillips'* translation reads, "'*I belong to the Lord, body and soul,' replied Mary, 'let it happen as you say'*" The stage was set. A woman past child-bearing age was pregnant with the forerunner of the Christ, and an unmarried girl was pregnant with the Son of God, but no one knew it except God and four isolated persons on the earth.

Of course, this news was too great to be kept secret. Besides, Mary was a teenage girl and pregnant for the first time with a thousand questions she needed to ask. She could not risk talking with anyone in Nazareth, but Elizabeth in Hebron would understand. Even this was risky, however, for Elizabeth's husband, Zacharias, was the priest who under the provision of the Law would be responsible for examining her and ordering her execution.

The impulsiveness of youth, plus the intense need to share her glorious secret, drove Mary to take the calculated risk, and she set off on the two-day journey to the priestly city. This in itself was a definite testimony to her innocence of any wrongdoing, for a guilty person would hardly rush to the home of the presiding judge to confess her condition to the judge's wife while preparing to stay in that home for three months. There would be no way for the ladies to keep the secret between themselves. There comes a time when pregnancy can no longer be concealed.

Mary and Elizabeth Rejoice Together

Bolstered by the angelic announcement that Elizabeth, too, was pregnant by action of God's grace to this priestly couple, Mary headed for the hill country of Judah (which means *praise*) and to Hebron, the city the tribe of Judah had given to the priests in the days of Joshua.

Worshipers of all ages have felt secure and comfortable among those who live in the mountains of praise. Praisers are less legalistic in their approach to God. They have found that relationship with God transcends the rules of religion, and they refuse to participate in anything that would hinder that relationship.

Those who dwell in Hebron (a city of refuge which means *alliance*), among the tribe of Judah (*praisers*), usually enjoy a life whose borders are narrower than those who govern themselves by rigid law. Their life of relationship with God is so joyful that they are unaware of the controls that love imposes upon them. Like the happily married woman, who so enjoys her family that she doesn't even think about the freedom she has sacrificed, so worshipers don't count the cost; they revel in the privileges.

Mary headed for Hebron, and when she found the correct address she *"entered the house of Zacharias and greeted Elizabeth. And it happened, when Elizabeth heard the greeting of Mary, that the babe leaped in her womb; and Elizabeth was filled with the Holy Spirit"* (Luke 1:40-41, NKJV). So mighty was the presence of Christ in Mary that both Elizabeth and the baby in her womb reacted in jubilation. The baby leaped and Elizabeth was filled with the Holy Spirit. Did Mary need any further confirmation?

In the fresh inspiration of being filled with the Holy Spirit, Elizabeth sang a beautiful beatitude to Mary: *"Blessed are you among women, and blessed is the fruit of your womb! Blessed is she who believed, for there will be a fulfillment of those things which were told her from the Lord"* (Luke 1:42, 45, NKJV).

The aged woman, who had lived a life in scrupulous observance of the Law and all its rituals, pronounced a blessing upon the young woman who would soon give birth to the One who would usher in the New Covenant. There was no jealousy and no contending to maintain the status quo. Elizabeth spontaneously rejoiced in the spirit for God's great provision, for how could there be a Messiah without change?

Mary's Magnificat

Mary's secret was out in the open. Since Elizabeth knew, it would now be safe to talk about it, but mere talk was not what came from Mary's lips. Such immediate and anointed confirmation of the angel's message caused her to explode into a psalm of rejoicing that rivals anything recorded in the Psalter. She sang or chanted:

> *"My soul glorifies the Lord and my spirit rejoices in God my Savior,*
>
> *for he has been mindful of the humble state of his servant. From now on all generations will call me blessed,*
>
> *for the Mighty One has done great things for me holy is his name.*
>
> *His mercy extends to those who fear him, from generation to generation.*
>
> *He has performed mighty deeds with his arm; he has scattered those who are proud in their inmost thoughts.*
>
> *He has brought down rulers from their thrones but has lifted up the humble.*
>
> *He has filled the hungry with good things but has sent the rich away empty.*
>
> *He has helped his servant Israel, remembering to be merciful to Abraham and his descendants forever, even as he said to our fathers."*
>
> (Luke 1:46-55)

The loveliness of this Magnificat has attracted generation after generation of worshipers, and its beauty is felt as intensely today as in any previous age of the Church. Yet it was composed and initially sung by a poor, simple peasant maid who was untrained in the culture that generally precedes the composition of a hymn so exquisitely perfect and so beautiful as this one.

How could Mary express such profound truth in this elegant manner? In herself she could never have done it, but she was only a channel for this hymn. Mary was undoubtedly taught it by inspiration of the Holy Spirit. Within her was a thought too large for utterance, but also within her was the very person of God, and the Spirit gave her a vocal release to express the truth that was within her womb. Like Isaiah, her lips were touched with a live coal from God's altar of worship. In perfect language, they gave expression to the perfect music of her sanctified inner nature as it thrilled under the touch of the Holy Spirit. Jesus had hardly been conceived when He became the inspiration of and the inspirer of true worship. As He would later tell the woman at Jacob's well, *"The water that I shall give him will become in him a fountain of water springing up into everlasting life"* (John 4:14, NKJV).

This fountain of the Holy Spirit was certainly springing forth from Mary. It was proof that Christ within her was illuminating her intellect, communicating fervor to her heart, and acting mightily on her will. And why not? Should not Mary be the first to taste the reality of the Incarnation? Mary looked within herself and exclaimed, *"My soul magnifies the Lord, and my spirit has rejoiced in God my Savior"* (Luke 1:46-47, NKJV).

She looked within—not around, not above, but within— and the eyes of her understanding, enlightened by the Spirit of God, fell upon the wondrous vision of the indwelling Babe. Understandably, as she looked on the presence of Jesus Christ dwelling within her, her whole being thrilled with a joy none before her had ever experienced. Others had seen visions of God, had walked and talked with God, had worked and spoken for God, but Mary had God dwelling in her womb. She was Christopheros—the Christ-bearer—and her song was about this wonderful indwelling Christ.

Rejoicing Worship Announces Jesus

What a contrast this outburst of joyful song was to the rituals of worship that were common to the Old Testament. So much of the old form of worship was taken with sacrifices, offerings, chantings, special robes, and burning of incense, for the dominant theme was propitiation of sin and appeasement of God. Occasionally there was a David who could rise in joyful response to God, but his kind were overshadowed with the theological thinkers to whom ritual and performance were both the beginning and the end of all religious observance.

Thank God for the young, the inexperienced, the nonreligious persons who, upon meeting Jesus, know nothing better than to rejoice in His presence and to extol His great grace. Every church needs new converts to infuse some life into its religion, for true worship is more than the formal recitation of a prepared creed; it is an informal release of the inner joy of relationship with Jesus Christ.

It was not by accident that God chose young Mary to be the mother of Jesus. She would enjoy Him in a rather nonreligious manner, and this was a far better atmosphere for Jesus' upbringing than in the home of a scribe or a priest who had become locked into ceremony, formality, ritual, or service. From the first days of her pregnancy, Mary was a worshiper of Jesus as a living person rather than an absent deity.

On the outer porch of the priest's house stood a representative of the old and the embodiment of the new. Amazingly, in the greatest event in the whole course of human history, the "stronger sex" had no part whatever. It involved Mary and God, and the first joyful response to the Incarnation came from the lips of two humble women who, in the Jewish religion of the day, would never have been allowed beyond the Court of the Women in the Temple.

Women have often been barred by men from the service of God, but God has repeatedly chosen women to enter into divine service that no man could or would perform. It seems almost humorous to hear men declare how unscriptural it is for women to proclaim Christ, when God Himself chose a woman to produce the body for Jesus Christ, and the first open proclamation of His presence came from two women who had inside information not available to any man.

It has often been pointed out that the New Testament contains just a few divine songs. It is therefore doubly interesting that the New Testament begins with two songs of praise brought forth by Elizabeth and Mary. Their lives were overflowing with faith and confidence in God that found expression in praise. This so aroused their slumbering powers that instead of two ordinary village women, we see two prophetesses and poetesses upon whom the Spirit of God abundantly rested and in whom faith was doing its transforming work.

Mary's Magnificat is a song of almost pure faith. Faith is a necessary prerequisite to joy, for the eye of the soul enables a person to discern the beauty, the excellency, and the glory of our unseen God. Faith views the reality, greatness, and certainty of the salvation and blessings that God has promised us. Mary placed God's promises before her mind, and she exalted God in them. In her voluminous praise, Mary made each divine attribute record God's glory in a new light. She extolled God's holiness, grace, power, justice, and beneficence.

The Magnificat is the first canticle or song of praise recorded in the New Testament, and it is a song of great joy. When Mary said, "*My spirit has rejoiced in God my Savior*" (Luke 1:47, NKJV), she used the word *agallido*, a rather remarkable Greek word for "rejoice." There is an Old English word taken from this Greek word which described a "gilliard," a certain exulting dance. It was a sort of leaping dance. Mary in effect declared, "*My spirit has danced like David before the ark—it has leaped and rejoiced in God my Savior.*"

Charles Spurgeon once said, "Some of my brethren praise God always in the minor key, or in the deep, deep bass; they cannot feel holy till they have the horrors." Mary's pattern for New Testament worship is superior: "*My spirit has rejoiced in God my Savior.*" We cannot rejoice too much in the Lord, for worship has its beginnings and finds it release and end in expressed joy.

Mary's Magnificat is glorious. It is full of faith, humility, and joy. It becomes the prelude to worship as Jesus taught it. He inspired and directed this praise from within these women, and this would prove to be the dividing line between Old and New Testament worship. When believers of the Old Covenant saw Jesus as the Messiah of God, they joyfully worshiped Him, just as believers of the New Covenant jubilantly worship Jesus now. At the initial appearance of Jesus, however, He was worshiped by a limited few.

2

Jesus Incarnate

Mary could rejoice before Jesus was born because she had "inside information." What her eyes could not see, her senses could relate to. God's promise was being fulfilled in her day by day. She did not need the baby in her arms to rejoice and praise God, for the message of the angel had been faithfully followed by conception and gestation. She knew that Jesus was on His way!

While Mary and Elizabeth were rejoicing, Joseph the espoused husband was mentally confused, emotionally hurt, and completely perplexed about what he should do. He didn't want to make Mary a public example and call for her execution, but neither did he feel that it was right for him to take her as his wife and raise the child of another man. He had almost decided to send her away to another community to let her have the baby secretly. *"But after he had considered this, an angel of the Lord appeared to him in a dream and said, 'Joseph son of David, do not be afraid to take Mary home as your wife, because what is conceived in her is from the Holy Spirit. She will give birth to a son, and you are to give him the name*

Jesus, because he will save his people from their sins" (Matthew 1:20-21).

Immediately Matthew, writing under the inspiration of the Spirit, added, *"All this took place to fulfill what the Lord had said through the prophet: 'The virgin will be with child and will give birth to a son, and they will call him Immanuel' which means, 'God with us.' "* (Matthew 1:22-23).

The Promise

In this brief angelic announcement to Joseph, we mortals were told that the Immanuel of the Old Testament and the Jesus of the New Testament are one and the same. Immanuel is the name of God incarnate, for Jesus the Savior is synonymous with Jehovah "I am."

The Apostle John wrote: *"The Word became flesh and made his dwelling among us. We have seen his glory, the glory of the One and Only, who came from the Father, full of grace and truth"* (John 1:14). It is unlikely that Joseph could understand this truth—something that had never been before was about to become. How could we expect him to understand the concept of God coming in the flesh?

As Frederick Buechner tells us in his book *Wishful Thinking*, "That is what incarnation means. It is untheological. It is unsophisticated. It is undignified. But according to Christianity it is the way things are" (page 43). We might add to this that the Incarnation is totally incomprehensible, not only to Joseph, but to us.

If we twentieth-century Christians, who have full access to the written New Testament, find it difficult to understand the Incarnation, try to imagine how Joseph must have felt. We are told that Joseph was *"a just man"* (Matthew 1:19, NKJV), so he must have had some training in the theology of the Jews. The Jewish position concerning God was and still is: *"Hear, O*

Israel: The LORD our God, the LORD is one!" (Deuteronomy 6:4, NKJV).

These were God's own Words to His people. In His dealings with Israel in her formative years, He was more severe in enforcing this truth than in anything else that He had taught them. The punishment for worshiping anything or anyone other than Jehovah was extreme. Repeatedly God spoke through the prophet Isaiah to remind His people, *"I am the LORD, and there is no other"* (Isaiah 45:18, NKJV). After the painful captivity in Babylon, the Jews remained monotheistic. There was no more overt idolatry among them.

With his synagogue training, Joseph had to know about Israel's succession of anointed prophets, priests, judges, and kings who had led the Hebrews into God's will through the generations, but none of these ever laid claim to being God. Even if they had, the failure of their humanity would have discredited them.

Furthermore, Joseph had been taught about Old Testament theophanic visitations where God came to men in the form of an angel, usually called *"the Angel of the LORD,"* or even in the likeness of another man as Abraham experienced before the destruction of Sodom and Gomorrah. This pronouncement by the angel, however, pictured more than God materializing as a human; it declared that God was actually becoming flesh. God Himself was becoming a man through the birth process, and He would inhabit the earth and fellowship with mortal men.

If theologians still stumble over this, how can we expect a humble carpenter to have understood it? There was no way Joseph could have comprehended this angelic proclamation; but he did, and then he obediently responded to it. In our approach to God, it is the obedience of faith, not the accuracy of our comprehension, that counts. Fortunately, the angel did not stipulate that Joseph's understanding or even his faith were qualifying factors.

Some things that are done by a sovereign God transcend and function independently of man's responses. By obediently taking Mary as his wife, Joseph was not permitting God to become a Man, for Christ was already in the womb of Mary; Joseph was merely accepting the opportunity to be a participant in this great mystery. No man's concepts can change the way God is, but they can be the factor that inhibits or releases God's presence.

When we accept the God of divine revelation, we enter into a personal relationship with Him that blesses both God and man, but our rejection of that revelation does not alter the facts of God Himself. Faith may change us, but it will not change God. God is Who He says He is, no matter what we may think He is.

The Process

As great as the promise of a resident Savior proved to be, the process of bringing us this Savior was even greater. Gabriel told Mary, "*You will be with child and give birth to a son, and you are to give him the name Jesus*" (Luke 1:31). It may well have been this same angel who told Mary's sweetheart not to fear taking her as his wife, for the conception was by divine action, and the Son Who would be born would be the Savior. The method of the conception was explained to Mary this way: "*The Holy Spirit will come upon you, and the power of the Most High will overshadow you. So the holy one to be born will be called the Son of God*" (Luke 1:35).

The Son of God—the Holy One—Jesus—Savior—Christ the Lord—the Immanuel, came to us through the birth process that is common to all humanity. His conception was of the Holy Spirit, His gestation was in Mary's womb, and His delivery was in a manger in Bethlehem. Heaven's crowned Prince became Mary's little child. The second person in the Godhead became the first baby in the life of a newly married young maiden.

The theological term for this is "Incarnation," which can be traced to the Latin version of John 1:14. The term refers to the conception, gestation, and birth of the Son of God as the Son of man, but it is extended to the whole experience of human life into which He entered, and it embraces the fact that Christ forever bears His humanity.

Both Matthew and Luke open with accounts of the miraculous conception of Jesus. John declares that "*the Word became flesh, and dwelt among us*" (John 1:14, NKJV), thereby saying what the Word previously was not flesh. Jesus was not simply a man in Whom the Logos took up residence. The Logos became man the incarnate Son of God. He Who was "*from the beginning*" entered into human history as a human participant in this history.

The Purpose

It would take a work larger than this entire book to adequately expound on the purpose of the Son of God becoming the Son of man, but there are at least three basic reasons for the Incarnation. Perhaps the most obvious reason for the birth of Jesus was to reveal the Father. Adam's sin separated the human race from the presence of Father God. Adam was driven out of the Garden, and in him all humanity fled from the presence of God.

Over the centuries, God's attempts at self-revelation have failed to bring men back to God. It was not until God became what we are, thereby removing the unapproachableness of the Father, that our fear of "the different" was removed and we were able to comfortably relate to the triune God.

Jesus repeatedly told us that He and the Father are one, and that the words He spoke were the words He heard the

Father speak, and the things He did were the things He saw the Father do. When Philip asked Jesus to reveal the Father to the disciples, "*Jesus answered: 'Don't you know me, Philip, even after I have been among you such a long time? Anyone who has seen me has seen the Father. How can you say, "Show us the Father?"'*" (John 14:9).

A second fundamental reason for the Incarnation was to reconcile us to God. Once sin was put away, there was no barrier outside of man to prevent a loving, living relationship with the Eternal God. Even though the Cross would bridge the gulf between the creature and the Creator, men had been independent of God for so long that they had no desire for Him.

Christ came to create a new craving for God. Paul expressed it this way: "*God sent the Spirit of his Son into our hearts, the Spirit who calls out, 'Abba, Father'*" (Galatians 4:6).

He, Whom we were once independent of, is now the longing of our hearts. Far from being competitive with Him, we now live with a craving for Him. Formerly we were bound in sin, but now our lives are bonded to Christ. We can't get along without His presence. All of this is because of the Incarnation.

A third foundational purpose for Christ's coming as a man is seen in the prologue to John's Gospel: "*The Word became flesh and made his dwelling among us. We have seen his glory, the glory of the One and Only, who came from the Father, full of grace and truth*" (John 1:14). This eternal person called "the Word" dwelled among us. He pitched His tent by us and came to live where we live. It is the figure of the Arab nation and of one who is going to take the same journey with us and be under the same rule with us. We are pilgrims through the world, and He came to join us in our pilgrimage.

Glorious as this concept is, John must have had an even loftier idea in using the word "tabernacled," for he was steeped in the Old Testament image of the Tabernacle in the Wilderness that became the basis for all Temple worship. Sometimes the Tabernacle was called the *"Tent of Meeting"* (Exodus 39:40), and other times it was called the *"tabernacle of the Testimony"* (Exodus 38:21).

If we would be a little more faithful to the Hebrew language and use the word "tent" in place of "Tabernacle," we might better understand it. It was the Tent of Meeting and the Tent of Testimony. When we read about the Tabernacle of the Congregation in the Old Testament, it does not mean that it was the place where men congregated for worship, but that it was the tent where God and man met for fellowship. The Tent of Meeting was the God-appointed place where He met with man and to which man came to meet with Him. Jesus is now this "Tent of Meeting." He is where God and man meet for fellowship.

Similarly, the Tent of Testimony did not mean that it was the place where men proclaimed the truth of God. The Tent of Testimony was the place where God spoke to men and men listened. In dwelling among us, Jesus became the Tent of Testimony through which God speaks to man.

We find God in Christ as we can find Him nowhere else. Christ became the speech after a long, long silence between God and man. God not only came down to us, but has joined Himself to His redeemed people, to our very beings, as individuals, and He has become, in Jesus, the place where we meet with God to commune and communicate with Him.

The Practicability

When Joseph obediently took Mary as his wife and journeyed with her to Bethlehem for the registration imposed upon them by Rome, he could not foresee that the baby born to Mary that night in the stable was the God-Man, but the

Church since then has consistently believed it. *"One Christ, true God, and true man"* has been her faith.

As instructed, Joseph named the baby, Jesus. When the fourfold Gospels came into the canon of the Scriptures, this God-Man is called *"Jesus"* nearly five-hundred times. Even the Gospel of John, which is admittedly the Gospel of our Lord's Deity, calls the Lord by the human name "Jesus" 247 times, almost half the number of times this name is used in the Gospels. The title *"Christ"* refers to His office. The designation *"Son of God"* refers to His person, but "Jesus" speaks of His humanity and availability.

In the shadow of a flickering lamp, Jesus Christ was born into this world and was called both "Jesus" and "Immanuel." This *"God with us"* baby immediately evoked worship. Before He could preach a sermon or perform a miracle, before He could speak or even understand what was happening around Him, Jesus became the object of worship because of His very person.

3

Jesus Investigated

The introductory promises of a coming God-man that were made to Mary, Joseph, Zacharias, and Elizabeth came to pass exactly as God had said they would, but it was all done quietly—almost secretly. It lacked fanfare or publicity. The initial excitement of conception gave way to the day-to-day problems of pregnancy and daily living.

Furthermore, Jesus was born at a confusing time. King Herod had required everyone to return to the city of his or her birth to be registered. It was a form of our IRS, only you could not file the tax by mail. Everyone was moving about. The griping of the populace could be heard everywhere. People were far too preoccupied to be concerned with the potential coming of Christ.

Even Mary and Joseph were deeply involved with marriage arrangements and setting up housekeeping. Mary was probably the only person with a perpetual awareness that Jesus was on His way. Every time the baby kicked in the womb, Mary remembered. Her morning sickness and aching back kept the promise in her conscious mind.

Babies don't seem to consult a calendar. When it is time to be born, they come whether it is convenient or not. Jesus was born during this tax upheaval that took Mary and Joseph from the home and nursery they had prepared for the baby. They had to make do with whatever they could find, for Jesus didn't arrive at a convenient time.

Angels announced the birth, and an unusual star appeared in the eastern sky that was further declaration of an unusual and supernatural event. These events had all Jerusalem talking. Someone had to investigate this to see if it was true.

Perhaps the most familiar verse in the entire Bible is: *"For God so loved the world that He gave His only begotten Son, that whoever believes in Him should not perish but have everlasting life"* (John 3:16, NKJV). Because the Old Testament is so taken up with God's dealings with the Jewish nation, and the New Testament centers around the Church, we sometimes mentally retranslate this verse to say, "God so loved the Jews and the Church," but it clearly states that God so loved the entire world and sent His Son to be the Savior of the whole world.

It should not seem strange to us, then, that men outside the Jewish covenants were searchers after God and even worshipers of God. In the time of Christ, there were scholars in the Eastern culture who seemed to be very familiar with the Scriptures of the Hebrews. They were, therefore, acquainted with the writings of the prophets who saw the Lord our God in various ways.

What admiration must have filled their hearts as they vicariously entered into the experiences of these great men of God's choosing. Through the eyes of the prophets, they saw God as radiantly beautiful with kingly majesty that crowned His deity, yet displaying graciousness and meekness—a meekness that was connected with His humanity, but did not take away from His majesty. What amazement these scholars must have felt as they viewed the prophets who, though seemingly overwhelmed with God's righteousness and truth, emphasized the gladness and joy of God's love when expounding on the divine nature. What a mighty God this is!

It would not be unusual for these seekers after truth to fall in love with such a wonderful person, for Peter, speaking of the Lord Jesus Christ, wrote, *"Though you have not seen him, you love him; and even though you do not see him now, you believe in him and are filled with an inexpressible and glorious joy"* (1 Peter 1:8).

The Start Of The Search

It is not beyond the realm of possibility that the search actually started many years before the birth of Jesus, when scholars came across the account of Balaam, the non-Hebrew prophet hired by Balak to curse Israel in the wilderness. This unusual account may have sent them to the books of Moses to see how Moses viewed the incident. In doing so, they delved further and further into the Old Testament.

In reading about Balaam and how God turned his desire to curse Israel into declarations of blessing, the Wise Men read Balaam's words: *"I see him, but not now; I behold him, but not near. A star will come out of Jacob; a scepter will rise out of Israel"* (Numbers 24:17). Accepting this as prophetic of a literal sign preceding the coming of the One

25

Whom Balaam saw in the distance, they charged their astronomers to watch for this new star.

The years of patient waiting and watching paid off; the star appeared. There was no mistaking it. This star had never been in the heavens before. Its magnitude was so great they could not have missed it. What they had seen declared in the Word was now displayed in the heavens. The written word had given them the "what" and "where" of this birth, but the sign in the sky told them "when."

God's marvelous truth and His exceedingly great promises are clearly spelled out on the pages of the Bible, but we usually need some spiritual vision, some supernatural occurrence, to make us aware that now is the time God intends to fulfill a promise to us. Without the quickening of the Holy Spirit, the Bible can remain as abstract truth, but when the Holy Spirit begins to confirm that truth with signs and wonders, we know the promise and the performance are about to get together.

It is to be expected that thousands of people saw this new star in the sky. Perhaps many of them sought a reason for it, but these Wise Men from the East already knew what it represented because they had been students of the Scriptures. He who neglects the Bible will never be a successful worshiper.

Years ago when I was taking flying lessons, my instructor told me that proper visual navigation moves from the map, upon which the course is charted, to the ground for confirmation. He said that whenever a pilot scanned the ground and then peered at his map, trying to find something that resembled the landscape, he was already lost. Similarly, when we look from the Word to the works of the Spirit, we are merely seeking confirmation of God's timing. When we move from supernatural demonstrations to the Word, trying to find an authority for it, it usually proves that we are already lost in our spiritual fog.

The search began in the Scriptures and proceeded into the heavens as they watched for the promised sign. The New Testament promises us, *"He will appear a second time, not to bear sin, but to bring salvation to those who are waiting for him"* (Hebrews 9:28, emphasis added). Even if the primary reference is to the Second Coming of Jesus, the principle is "look and see." It is not an accident that God seems to come to those who look for Him. It is an irrevocable principle of God.

The Scope Of The Search

Because Matthew says merely, *"Behold, there came wise men from the east to Jerusalem"* (Matthew 2:1, KJV), we are left with conjecture and tradition to fill in the blanks. The fact that King Herod in his anger ordered the execution of Bethlehem's children who were two years old and younger causes many to think that this star appeared at least two years before the actual birth of Christ and that these searchers arrived when Christ was still a baby. Others contend that the star would not have appeared until Christ was born and that these men arrived when Jesus was about two years old, which accounts for the statement that *"they saw the young Child"* (Matthew 2:11, NKJV) rather than "the Babe" whom the shepherds discovered.

Since the Bible is silent on this, we cannot speak with any certainty, but one thing is assured: their search was not a short, impetuous one. They spent two years on their trek. How much of this time was spent actually crossing the wilderness with their camel train is not known, but the general expression "from the East" would indicate that they traveled from a distant area.

Tradition proposes that these men came from different lands without prior communication with each other. They

27

presumably met in the wilderness while each thought he was on a solo expedition seeking the Jewish king. This suggests the fact that seldom does a group of persons unite to seek the Lord. Usually a deep yearning in an individual's heart causes him to start seeking God, and while in that search, others are found with the same longing, and they combine their efforts in seeking God. A common love unites the seekers for a common goal. It is like the love poem of Solomon: "*Draw me, we will run after thee*" (Song of Solomon 1:4, KJV). What starts as a singular action ends up as a plural response.

These Wise Men, called "astrologers" in the *Living Bible*, followed the trail of curiosity—searching with dedication, inquiry, and devotion—all because of a supernatural star. Their goal was to follow that star to Christ, and this is the purpose of any supernatural manifestation of God.

These seekers left home and country and set out across the trackless desert with nothing but the star to guide them. Obviously this entailed hardships and was filled with insecurity and questions, but they continued until they reached their goal.

Subsequent seekers after Christ have had similar experiences, for those hungry for Jesus frequently find that they must leave the familiar surroundings of their religious heritage and experience the loneliness of the desert for a season. Moses had a lengthy season of desert life, and Paul spent at least three years in the Arabian desert after his conversion. Sometimes God uses the isolation of the desert to let some of the old concepts drain out of our lives before He fills us with the newness of His presence.

It is likely that many of the preconceived ideas of these Wise Men were tempered or totally discarded by the time they arrived in Jerusalem. It is equally probable that interaction with each other not only strengthened their faith, but enlarged their vision. God usually gives progressive revelation to His people. As we move out in faith on what He has given, He will give us more. Furthermore, He loves to give different parts of the puzzle to separate individuals so that in their sharing with each other, they begin to form a larger part of the picture. Worshipers need one another far more than they realize.

The desert of man-made religion can make the search for Jesus difficult. It harbors marauders who would like to get their hands on the special gifts that worshipers bear in their search for Jesus. It also holds special oases of worship, but God is not the object of that worship. These places of small springs and a few palms have their share of advisers who have never seen what the Wise Men saw, nor have they ever known a hunger for anything beyond their desert mirage.

The attendants of these oases will do their best to convince the seeker that there is nothing greater than their oasis. To prove it, they point out the great contrast between the oasis and the wilderness around it, but wise men know better. They have seen the truth in the Word that has been confirmed by actions in the spiritual realms, and no tiny spring in the desert will ever satisfy them.

No prestige, honor, position, or commission would satisfy these Wise Men who were seekers after Christ, and compared to Him, nothing else mattered. What they left behind to begin their search was far better than anything they could find in a tiny oasis.

The Surprise Of The Search

When the star led the men to the land of Israel, they thought their quest was over, but the truth was that their surprises had just begun. Some tradition tells us that these men were kings which, if true, helps us to understand their concept that the star pointed to a newborn king, and helps us to know why they found an immediate audience with Herod. There was no more logical place to look for a new king than at the seat of authority and government, but Jesus was not there.

Many seekers have been disappointed to discover that Jesus is not located in their denominational headquarters. Jesus later told Pilate, *"My kingdom is not of this world"* (John 18:36). Worshipers will have to look beyond church government to find the true Object of their affections, for the King is not in an earthly palace.

By inquiry in Jerusalem, the Wise Men also learned that Jesus wasn't in the Temple. Although He was taken there for circumcision when He was eight days old, only two elderly people recognized Him as the Christ. Everyone else, including the priests, were so caught up in the ceremonies, rituals, sacrifices, and offerings prescribed by God as expressions of worship that they failed to recognize the Object of worship when He was in their midst.

Religion often gets too busy serving Jesus to actually have any time for Him. It is shocking how seldom Jesus goes to church anymore. Maybe He's tired of being ignored by the "worshipers."

A third great surprise for these seekers was the discovery that Jesus wasn't even in the holy city of Jerusalem. In David's day, Jerusalem was visualized as the symbol of God's presence among His people, but when God sent His people into Babylonian captivity, Ezekiel saw a vision of the glory of God departing from the Temple and leaving the city.

Jewish writers of later times declared that among the things missing in the rebuilt Temple of Ezra's day was the Shekinah of God's presence. They admitted that there was never again a demonstration of God's glory either in the Temple or in the city. As that angel testified at the empty tomb after Christ's resurrection, *"He is not here"* (Matthew 28:6).

Having troubled Herod and all Jerusalem with the unanswered question, "Where is the King?" the Wise Men decided to return to square one and follow the star. Mercifully, it led them to the Christ-Child. When they did find Jesus, He was in a simple house in the humble village of Bethlehem. God's glory no longer needed the pompous palace or the sacraments of the Temple, for God had chosen to demonstrate His glory in His Son—*"God . . . has in these last days spoken to us by His Son . . . the brightness of His glory and the express image of His person"* (Hebrews 1:1-3, NKJV). This Son cannot always be found where He is expected, but wherever He is found, He is the instant object of worship.

The Satisfaction Of The Search

There was no worship during the seeking—only wonder and talk of worship. Worship can be performed only in the presence of our God. One look at Jesus evoked such a spirit of wonder, awe, reverence, praise, and thanksgiving that these Wise Men immediately prostrated themselves in homage before Him and worshiped Him. Perhaps they realized what we often ignore: Because of our limited spiritual understanding, our worshiping moods do not last long. We need to respond quickly to any inspiration of the Spirit to worship Jesus.

The palace with all its power did not inspire the worship of these seekers. Even the great Temple of God, with its beautiful forms of worship that had been given to the Jews by God Himself, could not bring these men to their knees. They ignored all these things and said, "We have come to worship Him."

Perhaps they were able to respond directly to God in Jesus because they were not preconditioned to think that God could be approached only through the priesthood and Temple rituals. Those without prior religious training quite frequently respond to a revelation of Jesus with a higher level of worship than those who were raised in the Church. They do not have to fight their way through the barriers that religion tends to raise to impede our worship of Jesus.

The Wise Men came prepared to worship as they carried gifts with them, but they did not say, "We have come to present gifts." No! They came to worship Him. The gifts were but a means of expressing their worship to Jesus. These were learned men of high rank and privilege. They were accustomed to having men travel great distances to see them, and perhaps they had done the same thing in order to see other great men of their day. But here in the simple peasant home, they didn't say that they had traveled for many months to see the new King; they declared that the whole purpose of their visit was to worship Him.

In looking for the word "worship" in the Old Testament, we have to cover seventeen chapters of Genesis before we discover the Hebrew word *schachah* (worship), but when we open the New Testament, we find the word "worship" on the first page. Tradition says that there were three Wise Men. If this is true, we have a reversal from the first time the word "worship" occurs in the Old Testament when God appeared to Abraham as three men. The great patriarch responded by prostrating himself and saying, "*My LORD, if I have now found favor in Your sight . . .*" (Genesis 18:3, NKJV).

To Abraham, the three were one, for he recognized this as God appearing in human form. In the Matthew account, three (we presume) men recognized God in a single human form and bowed to worship Him. In both Testaments, worship is the response of persons coming into the immediate presence of God as He appeared in human form.

What seems improper, however, is that the word "worship" in the New Testament describes the actions of persons who were outside the covenant God made with Israel, men whom the Jews considered "pagans." Later, Christ's greatest discourse on worship was given to a Samaritan, a race the Jews loathed so deeply that they wouldn't even speak to one of them.

Beyond proving that Jesus came as the Savior of the world, surely this also establishes that worship is never based upon the worth of the worshiper. Jesus was worshiped because of Who He was, not because of who they were. None of us will ever be sufficiently worthy to worship Jesus, but He is always worthy of our worship, and He never rejects worship that flows from an honest heart.

They came—they saw—they worshiped. This will always be the order of worship: first, the search for Him; second, the sight of Him; and third, the satisfaction of pouring out our deep love and adoration for Him. He is worth the search, for there is none higher than our Lord Jesus Christ on all the earth or in the heavens above.

Perhaps none of us will fully realize the importance of worship in God's sight until we reach heaven as glorified beings and are in Christ's presence continuously. Then, when the full knowledge of what a glorious Being He is floods our souls and we more clearly understand His worthiness, His glory, His beauty, and the great love He has for us, we will likely wonder why we missed the great joy of worshiping Him more while we were here on the earth.

We need the spirit of adventure these wise men possessed. We need to investigate Jesus, for when we discover that He is all He claims to be, and all the Scriptures declare Him to be, we will worship. It is almost impossible to see God in Jesus without responding in worship.

4

Jesus' Inauguration

Every four years as our elected president takes the oath of office, the victorious political party puts on an elaborate inaugural ball of such proportions that it fills much of Washington D.C. In countries with a monarchy, the coronation of a king or queen is a state affair with dignity, pageantry, pomp, and ceremony. The purpose is to confer dignity and honor on the new ruler, and to inform the world that he or she is now in power.

Wouldn't we expect God to have some sort of inauguration for the coming of His Son into the world? After all, He came as the *"Lord of lords and King of kings"* (Revelation 17:14). God did have a coronation or an inauguration for Jesus, but it was nothing like we might have expected. The Roman government was not informed, King

Herod was not invited, and the religious rulers of the day ignored the entire affair. Still, God found some special persons who were open to the fresh revelation that the Messiah had come. Their response to this inauguration celebration was worship. It always is. When He is high and lifted up, saints bow low in worship.

Speaking of Jesus, Paul proclaimed, *"Therefore God exalted him to the highest place and gave him the name that is above every name, that at the name of Jesus every knee should bow, in heaven and on earth and under the earth, and every tongue confess that Jesus Christ is Lord, to the glory of God the Father"*(Philippians 2:9-11).

To us this is academic, but in the early Church this was the controversy that induced great persecution. The concept of the Trinity was unknown to Judaism. Worship of anyone short of God was seen as idolatry.

Then it happened, as announced by the angel Gabriel, that a Baby was born in a manger. Shepherds worshiped Him, Anna worshiped Him, Simeon worshiped Him, the Wise Men worshiped Him, the disciples worshiped Him, the formerly lame, blind, and leprous worshiped Him.

From Christ's conception to His crucifixion, it was never natural vision that caused people to worship Him—it was supernatural revelation that caused men and women to prostrate themselves before Him in humble worship. Worship is always a response to revelation, never the result of mere observation.

It is likely that hundreds, perhaps even thousands, of persons heard the report of the birth of Jesus, but only those who received a supernatural revelation responded in worship. God graciously chose to invite four classes of persons to the inauguration of His Son, and they worshiped Jesus.

The very first to know about the birth of Jesus were the humble peasants: Joseph and Mary, and then the shepherds.

The second class were the holy priests, represented in Zacharias and his wife, Elizabeth. The third class were the honored prophets Simeon and Anna. Finally, Christ was worshiped by heathen kings when the Wise Men followed the star to Jerusalem. These were the honored guests at Christ's inauguration ceremony.

Participation of Shepherds in the Inauguration

Tradition suggests that the shepherds, to whom the angels announced the birth of Christ, were in the employ of the priests of the Temple at Jerusalem. They raised the sheep that would be used in the ritualistic sacrifices of Judaism. As they huddled around a small campfire, trying to keep warm in the chill of the night hours while still remaining alert to any sound a predator might make in approaching their flocks, they were startled by a blazing light that made the night as bright as day.

When their eyes had painfully adjusted to this sudden change in the intensity of light, they saw before them an angel of the Lord who said, "*Do not be afraid. I bring you good news of great joy that will be for all the people. Today in the town of David a Savior has been born to you; he is Christ the Lord. This will be a sign to you: You will find a baby wrapped in cloths and lying in a manger*" (Luke 2:10-12).

What an announcement this was and to what an audience! One wonders why this "*multitude of the heavenly host praising God and saying: 'Glory to God in the highest, and on earth peace, good will toward men!'*" (Luke 2:13-14, NKJV) didn't go directly to the high priest in Jerusalem. It seems almost a waste for beings of such dignity to be sent to men of such low degree. What could they do with so vast a revelation?

The Gospels offer no answer to the first question, but Luke fully answers the second one. Some have suggested that the angels did, indeed, try to communicate with the religious leaders in Jerusalem, but were unable to get through to them. If this should prove to be true, it would certainly be consistent with the fact that we are often so occupied with religious matters that we are deaf and blind to spiritual truth.

Merely maintaining the memory of past revelations can desensitize us to the spiritual realm until God's voice and His messengers, the angels, are as foreign to us as they are to pagans. **To have heard what God said may not qualify us to hear what God is saying.**

The reason the shepherds should receive so magnificent an angelic visitation is totally unknown to us, but what they did with that visitation is clearly stated. They left their flocks and went to investigate. Finding the angelic message to be correct, *"The shepherds returned, glorifying and praising God for all the things they had heard and seen, which were just as they had been told"* (Luke 2:20). The angelic visitation provoked a response that led them into praising God.

Worshipers do not always come from the ranks of the learned and the religious. Jesus, quoting Psalm 8, said, *"Have you never read, 'From the lips of children and infants you have ordained praise'?"* (Matthew 21:16). It is our response, never our rank, that makes worshipers out of us. If we will listen to the message God has sent to us, whether by angel, by preacher, or by reading the Bible, it will bring us to Jesus and we will worship.

The specific revelation given to the shepherds was *"a Savior is born."* We don't know whether they associated this message with the lambs they were raising. From our perspective, it seems fitting that those who tended the sheep that were offered as a type of the coming Lamb of God should be among the first to meet God's Savior.

The shepherds of God's lambs should always be the first to meet the Lamb of God. Meeting the Savior is a prerequisite for worship, for until our sin has been remitted to Jesus, we are so separated from God that we cannot worship. Once we, too, have the revelation that *"there is born to you this day . . . Savior, who is Christ the Lord,"* worship becomes an automatic response to Jesus. New converts worship with a rejoicing enthusiasm that causes them to emulate the shepherds in taking their expression of love for Jesus into their daily lives, and sharing it with anyone they meet. Joy comes from Jesus, and they have just met Him as their Savior.

The order of the shepherds' worship experience seems to have been revelation, response, rejoicing, and reporting. Similarly, when we hear what God is saying and hearken with obedient response, we will experience a new happiness in life that will cause us to herald the news automatically everywhere we go.

Worship does not need religious trappings to be vital; it needs only a fresh revelation of a Savior. In the saving work of Jesus, He has restored to us what Adam forfeited for us: authority under God, relationship with God, the peace of God, and worship responses to God. Without this redeeming restoration, worship is difficult. Prisoners under the law wail rather than worship. Slaves of the religious systems petition God rather than praise Him, but restored sons of God revel in His promises, rejoice in His Person, and respond worshipfully in His presence.

Simeon's and Anna's Participation in the Inauguration

Worship requires coming into God's presence. We may praise from a distance, but we worship only when we are in the presence of God. When Jesus was only eight days old, He was taken into the Temple at Jerusalem to be circumcised to fulfil the law of Moses. It is interesting and perhaps quite consistent with modern-day experience, that only two persons in the multitude of people in the Temple recognized Him as the Christ. Simeon and Anna looked down the long line of newborn infants awaiting circumcision and saw the promised Messiah in the baby, while even the officiating priests failed to discern this.

Their sight was not a result of the "gift of suspicion." It was divine illumination that caused them to recognize the divine presence, and this is as needed today as it was then. Without heavenly illumination, we may well be in the very midst of the Holy presence and not know it.

Religion and religious leaders frequently fail to recognize major moves of God until the outpouring has passed into the history books, and then it is too late to become a part of the visitation. Too often the presence of God is missed because it does not come in the way we thought it would come. God's presence is in the darkness as well as in the light. It is in pain as well as in pleasure. While it is true that God is everywhere present, it is equally true that He is rarely recognized, appreciated, or apprehended—for most of us live lives that are blinded to His presence.

These two prophets who visualized God in the waiting line of worshipers were persons of high spiritual character. Anna, a prophetess, had been married for seven years and by the time of Jesus' birth had been a widow for eighty-four years. If she was just a teenager when she married, she would have been over a hundred years old. For the preceding eighty or more years *she never left the temple but worshiped night and day, fasting and praying*" (Luke 2:37).

This voluntary cloistering of herself unto the service of God released her from all worldly cares and kept her attention centered upon God. Her lifestyle opened her to receive the

40

prophetic word that proceeded from the lips of Simeon, and she saw God in Jesus. How easy it is to tag as "radicals" those persons who give much of their lives to worshiping and serving Jesus. It is usually these "radicals" who get a glimpse into what God is about to do.

Dr. Luke told us considerably more about Simeon than he did about Anna. The Gospel record says, "*Now there was a man in Jerusalem called Simeon, who was righteous and devout. He was waiting for the consolation of Israel, and the Holy Spirit was upon him*" (Luke 2:25). The revelation of God in Christ Jesus came to Simeon through the indwelling Spirit—not through a star, an angel, or even the angel chorus. It was his character—what he actually was in God—that made him open to a revelation.

We are told that Simeon was "*just*." The Greek word is *dikaios*, which means "equitable in character, innocent, holy, or righteous." Simeon's horizontal relationships were transparent. He lived in honesty with his fellow man. He was right in his actions, right in his attitudes, and right in his relationships. Whether we like it or not, our home life, business life, social life—in short, our "natural life"—greatly affects our spiritual vision.

Cornelius was visited by God because of his righteous life, and so were many others. There can be no great division between our natural and spiritual life; we walk by one set of rules. Holiness and righteousness must be manifested everywhere and at all times.

We are also told that Simeon was "devout." His vertical relationship was keen and clean. He was not content with merely being righteous with his fellow man; he sought after God. His devotion was based on commitment. It is great to love life and love our fellow man, but we were created to love God. Revelation of God comes to those whose horizontal and vertical relationships are good.

Luke also mentioned that Simeon was *"waiting for the consolation of Israel"* (Luke 2:25). He was not unduly caught up in the negatives of his "now" life. Roman captivity did not dull his anticipation of a divine government under the promised Messiah. He allowed his "now" life to be affected by the future life. He came from the Word to reality, not from reality to the Word.

We, too, must learn to let the supernatural deeply affect the natural if we would see God. Our present life needs to be *"hidden with Christ in God"* (Colossians 3:3) so that *"when Christ, who is your life, appears, then you also will appear with him in glory"* (Colossians 3:4).

It was also said of Simeon that *"the Holy Spirit was upon him."* Simeon was still living under the Old Covenant long before the outpouring of the Spirit on the Day of Pentecost, and yet he was already experiencing a life full of God's Spirit. Though out of his dispensation, he was endued with the divine presence.

"Just, devout, waiting" persons need not accept the limitations of present revelations or dealings. The glories of the future are available to men in the present, for God and His ways are timeless. Every season of God's dealings with men has been preceded by one or more persons who advanced into it ahead of the others. God has "forerunners" for every move; even today.

Simeon was not awaiting a divine revelation; he walked in such a revelation, for *"it had been revealed to him by the Holy Spirit that he would not die before he had seen the Lord's Christ"* (Luke 2:26). God's Word had been made alive to him. God's promises had been personalized, and he lived his life in the light of that quickened Word.

This was more than a desire, ambition, hope, or spiritual hallucination—Simeon had a promise of revelation. He did not plead it; he just waited for it. This waiting covered many years, but he finally saw the Lord. He who walks in the Spirit will not miss the fulfillment of God's promises. Paul said that Abraham was, *"fully persuaded that God had power to do what he had promised. This is why 'it was credited to him as righteousness'"* (Romans 4:21-22). By divine action, God said the same thing about Simeon, and it is something that God would like to say of us.

Because of a righteous life that believed God, Simeon saw the Lord. As a result of that revelation, Simeon worshiped the Lord. He *"blessed God."* The Greek word is *eulogeo*—he eulogized God. He bragged on God and expressed high praise for God. The revelation of the indwelling Spirit brought Simeon to a higher level of worship than that of the shepherds or the Wise Men. The deeper the revelation, the higher the level of worship. The shepherds received the revelation of a Savior and they rejoiced. Simeon received a revelation of the Christ, and he eulogized God.

Worship has always been a response to a revelation of the person of Christ. Perhaps we need less emphasis on the methods of worship and more emphasis on the Person to whom we give our worship.

Some years ago, I had brought my congregation to a level of response to God beyond which I could not take them. I preached on praise and worship, and we exercised praise and worship, but we could not rise any higher than we were. One day the Lord spoke to me, "Your people are already responding to Me to the extent of their comprehension of Me. If you can help them see Me in greater measure, they will respond to Me in higher measure."

For the next year I stopped preaching on praise and worship and just preached on God. As it turned out, God was right. As we saw God high and lifted up, our response to God also lifted higher and higher, because worship is always a response to a revelation. Fresh revelations produce fresh worship responses, and higher revelations bring higher responses.

God is all we have seen Him to be—and much more. We can never exhaust the revelation He has given of Himself in the Word. When the indwelling Spirit quickens the written Word, like Isaiah, we see *"the Lord seated on a throne, high and exalted, and the train of his robe filled the temple"* (Isaiah 6:1). We will worship God at a level higher than we have ever been able to reach before in our response to Him.

God seldom gives a complete revelation in an instant of time. Most revelations begin with something startling like an angel, a star, a miracle, or an inner voice. It is only the person who is willing to pursue this embryonic truth—this "teaser"— who comes into the full revelation God is prepared to give.

The inauguration of Jesus was attended by few people, but each of them worshiped, for worship is almost an innate response to a revelation that *"Jesus Christ is Lord!"*

5

Jesus Initiated

Up to this point in the Gospels, Christ's role in worship was passive. As the baby, He was the object of worship. The Holy Spirit inspired that worship, and the Father received it as acceptable. Much can be learned about worship by merely observing the kind of worship to which God assents.

After Matthew introduced the word "worship" to describe the action of the Wise Men, the Gospels remain almost silent about the life of Jesus. We learn about His short sojourn into Egypt while awaiting the death of Herod, and we are told about the time He stayed behind in the Temple when He was about twelve years of age. The questions He asked the learned scholars that day astounded them, for He had a depth of spiritual perception far beyond His obvious age.

It is likely that the childhood days of Jesus were filled with frustration as He grappled with His dual nature. During the time when Joseph was teaching Jesus the carpentry trade, Jesus must have had a deep inner craving for something higher than mere manual labor. He knew He was not born to be a carpenter, but what exactly was His purpose on the earth?

He obviously had not understood any of Simeon's or Anna's prophecies in the Temple, since He was only eight days old when they were given, and there were no subsequent prophetic words to give Him guidance or confirmation. Even the teaching priests in the Temple had not given Him any satisfactory answers the day He questioned them. They did, however, heighten His anxiety to know Himself. By the time Jesus reached early manhood, He had an inner knowing that He was the God-man, but the first confirmation came as He stood near the Jordan River listening as John, His cousin, preached. Without fanfare or buildup, John stopped preaching long enough to point his weathered finger at Jesus and proclaim, *"Look, the Lamb of God, who takes away the sin of the world! . . . I have seen and I testify that this is the Son of God"* (John 1:29, 34).

The Confirmation

Responding to this, Jesus submitted to John's water baptism, although He had to deal with John's protests of unworthiness. *"As soon as Jesus was baptized, he went up out of the water. At that moment heaven was opened, and he saw the Spirit of God descending like a dove and lighting on him. And a voice from heaven said, 'This is my Son, whom I love; with him I am well pleased'"* (Matthew 3:16-17).

Since the Mosaic law taught that two or three witnesses certified a matter beyond further question, Jesus now had the ultimate confirmation. He had John's anointed testimony, the testimony of the Spirit that rested upon Him, and the testimony of the Father's voice from heaven. It was settled. He was, as He had supposed, the Son of God. His divine identity was assured and announced.

This was more than a time of declaration. It was initiation time. Jesus was about to be initiated into His ministry on earth. First, He had to be assured of Who He was. Next, this assurance had to tested.

Matthew recorded that before Jesus had time to exult in this outer confirmation of an inner reality, "*Jesus was led by the Spirit into the desert to be tempted by the devil*" (Matthew 4:1). The English word "led" is actually too mild a translation of the original Greek word. "*Driven*" would probably be more accurate a word to use. This same Spirit that had descended upon Jesus in the form of a dove, now drove Him as a lion would force a prey to flee in fright before him. Jesus did not need the congratulations of people. He needed to be tested until this revelation was so certain within Himself that He would never doubt it, no matter how difficult life might become.

All new spiritual revelations are subject to testing. We are told that "*the testing of your faith develops perseverance,*" and "*Blessed is the man who perseveres under trial, because when he has stood the test, he will receive the crown of life that God has promised to those who love him*" (James 1:3, 12). Jesus—the perfect Man, our example, our High Priest, and the Lamb of God—had to be examined, tried, and tested before He was released into His ministry. So do we. It is part of our initiation ceremony!

Because of our common association of temptation with immorality, we do well to remind ourselves that the New Testament uses the exact same Greek word, *peirasmos*, for test, trial, and temptation. The word literally means, "putting to the test." From God's point of view, it is a test. From Satan's point of view, it is a temptation, and from the believer's point of view, it is a trial.

The purpose of the test is not to reveal our weaknesses, but to demonstrate the strength that God's Spirit has induced into our lives. Like the new product that is sent to a laboratory for extensive testing before the guarantee period can be determined, so there are times when God seems to deliver us to the "tormentor" to demonstrate, both to us and to the spiritual world, just how great a measure of His grace has been extended to us.

The Tempter

The passive role of Jesus in worship was about to end. Having been declared by the Father to be the Son of God, His responses to the Father would either be worship responses or rebellious refutations. He Who had been the worshiped One was about to be challenged to become the worshiper. The person chosen by God to conduct this test was introduced for the first time in the New Testament under the titles of "tempter" and "devil." Jesus and the devil were certainly not unknown to each other. It was the creature tempting the Creator to disbelieve the clear declaration of God.

The devil was challenging Jesus to doubt the fact that He was the Son of God. Twice the tempter said, *"If You are the Son of God . . ."* (Matthew 4:3, 6, NKJV), and then he suggested something that Jesus could do to prove that He was Who God said He was. Jesus seemed to know that our faith is already in danger if we have to do something dramatic to prove it, for God's Word rests upon His nature, not upon our demonstration of spiritual energy.

In many Christian circles there is unfortunate confusion as to the nature and work of the devil. Perhaps Christians have gained too many of their concepts of the devil from ancient Greek mythology and religious art. They picture the devil as having horns, cloven hoofs, a forked tail, running around in red underwear, and using a pitchfork to prod Christians while daring them to try the pleasures of sin. This is an absolute and cunning deception. Paul tells us, *"Satan himself masquerades as an angel of light"* (2 Corinthians 11:14).

By coupling Isaiah 14, Ezekiel 28, and Revelation 12, we get quite a composite picture of the one whose name in heaven was Lucifer. He was magnificent, beautiful, and radiant with the glory of God. He held high position as an archangel, and he was the anointed cherub who covered the Ark of the Covenant. The book of Job indicates that Lucifer was in charge of the music in heaven, and so he was probably in charge of heaven's worship. He was the object of God's love and trust, but he exalted himself up in pride and purposed to replace God.

God instructed Michael and his angels to cast Lucifer and his angels out of heaven, and they came from heaven to use the earth for their headquarters. Nothing changed in Lucifer except his geographic location. He still strives to replace God as the object of worship, and man became his special target.

Rather than a vile being, as we consider vileness, Satan is a very religious being who understands worship far better than we mortals do, for he got all his worship training in heaven under the guidance of Father God. He is still far more interested in worship than in sin. He is more likely to be in church than in the worst den of iniquity in any area. This fallen angel would rather pervert a person's worship than corrupt his morals, for he knows that if he can defile our worship, we will corrupt our morals ourselves.

The Temptation

When Satan was assigned the contract to test Jesus, he included worship in the test. In the Matthew account of the first temptation, during the forty days when Jesus went without sleep and food, the devil challenged Jesus to use His position as the Son of God to make bread out of stones. "Satisfy Your physical needs with Your spiritual energy" was the basis of this test. It is still among the temptations the devil uses against the chosen as servants of God.

"Use spiritual gifts to make money" is the nature of the test today. All spiritual gifts have commercial value, but no spiritual gift has been given for that purpose. Jesus later taught, *"Freely you have received, freely give"* (Matthew 10:8). God's free gifts should never be commercialized by gifted individuals.

The second temptation was concerned with drawing attention to Jesus. The devil challenged Him to jump off a high pinnacle of the Temple and land as softly as a feather.

"Grandstand your spiritual gifts" is the modern counterpart. It's the temptation to show off what you can do and watch the crowd gather. We need to remember that if we draw a crowd by jumping, every time we have a crowd, they will call for us to jump. They will not be interested in Jesus— just in the jump.

The third temptation was vital, for it did not involve Christ's abilities, it concerned His attitudes. The devil challenged Jesus to worship him (Lucifer) in exchange for anything in the world He wanted. The tempter has always offered things for worship, but Jesus wasn't interested in "things." He had come to redeem men. Perhaps if the modern Church were less interested in things and more interested in people, the devil would have less power over it.

In handling this final temptation to pervert His worship by paying homage to a rebellious creature instead of worshiping a loving Father God, Jesus quoted an Old Testament passage (Exodus 34:14) and applied it in such a way as to establish three abiding principles of worship:

1. The priority of worship—worship first, service second.
2. The exclusivity of worship—worship God only.
3. The energy of worship—it resists the devil.

Temptation's Answer: A Principle

The answer to temptation is never emotion. How we feel is useless when facing the enemy. With faith we must respond to his taunts and tests to be disobedient, and faith demands a Bible principle for its foundation. Jesus had already learned this. He knew that if the Scriptures stated it, that settled it. The Father's Word always took priority over Satan's word.

The first and most obvious of these principles is the priority that Jesus established for worship. He told the devil, *"Worship the Lord your God, and serve him only"* (Matthew 4:10). Worship first—service second. Response to relationship comes first, response to needs is second. As difficult as it may be for religious people to accept, we are not "saved to serve"—we are saved to worship! God did not redeem slaves into His service at Calvary; He restored sons into fellowship with the Father.

In the thirty years I served as a pastor, it was my observation that persons who are works oriented are seldom worshipers, for they substitute their actions for expression of their attitudes. They would rather work for God than worship Him. Service is not wrong, but if it is a substitute for what God requests, it will likely know the curse of God, for although

God often blesses supplements, He never blesses substitutes. Worship of God is the ultimate service in heaven, so it should at least be the beginning service on earth. Frankly, until we do the worship "thing," we cannot do anything that is of any spiritual value.

While it is rare for worship to proceed from service, it is normal for service to flow out of worship. Worshipers are often the most active workers in the kingdom of God, for their service is an expression of their love for God, very much as the service in a loving marriage becomes an expression of that love.

Most women learn early in life that men have difficulty expressing their inner feelings to a woman, especially in communicating his love for her. However, I have never heard of a young man who, in spite of all his hang-ups, approached the object of his affections and asked her to become his maid, cook, and the mother of his children. His offer, in all certainty, would be rejected.

If, however, he first laid the foundation of their relationship with love and trust, he would not have to ask his wife to do anything. She would willingly see to his needs in a spirit of love, and she would expect him to do the same. They happily serve one another in physical demonstrations of love; not because they have to, but because they want to.

The Response

The Bible does not teach that God sent a worklist to earth and offered salvation to those who would fulfill the requirements. What we do read is that "*God demonstrates his own love for us in this: While we were still sinners, Christ died for us*" (Romans 5:8).

God draws us to Himself in a loving embrace and assures us of His deep affection for us. Such dynamic and divine love so overwhelms us that we find ourselves—very much like Isaiah—volunteering to do anything He wants done. Worshiping Christians serve God as a concrete and continued expression of their love for Him.

Real worship is, among other things, the expression of a feeling we have about Jesus. It resides in our hearts and must find an expressive outlet. We can serve God without this feeling, but we cannot worship Him without it, for worship is love responding to love, not service responding to need.

A. W. Tozer once said, "Men can have two kinds of love for God: the love of gratitude, or the love of excellence." So much of our worship seems to be a response of gratitude. We pay homage for a gift received or we worship because of a work accomplished by God. While this is not wrong, it is very limited. We humans are so constructed that we cannot maintain the feeling of gratitude for a protracted season. We can remember the action for a lifetime, but we cannot reenter the emotion of gratitude we felt at the time of the action. If worship is the expression of a feeling we have for God, then substituting memory for feeling will not work; it will lead us into ritual rather than into real worship.

Trying to remember the feeling you had forty years ago when Jesus saved you from sin is like an adult trying to remember the feeling of natural birth. The fact is obvious, but the feeling is obliterated. If Christians insist upon responding to God in worship based upon their gratitude for His actions, they had better be certain that God has done something recently, for that feeling of gratitude will not remain.

In my traveling ministry, I get my share of compliments. People tell me that they love my ministry, have been blessed by my tapes, and have been inspired by my books—which is my favorite compliment, since writing is the hardest work I do. On a recent occasion when my wife Eleanor and I were having one of those heart-to-heart talks most couples get around to about once a year, she said to me, "Judson, I don't love you for your ministry or for your books. I love you! I loved you before you had a ministry, and if something would take your ministry away from you, I would love you just the same."

That one statement meant more to me than all the hundreds of compliments I had received before it. There is someone who loves me for who I am, not for what I do. That is undergirding and strength producing.

Perhaps today's Church needs to graduate from mere gratitude as the basis of our worship to the love of excellence. All Christians need a love of God just because He is God and because of the excellence of His character. This love becomes adoration which is the result not of being co-laborers, but of being companionate lovers of God.

The very first time Jesus met the issue of worship, He declared to the one who defiled worship in heaven, "Worship first—service second!" Historically, codified religion has ignored this priority by being far more service oriented than worship centered. However, it is not too late for the true Church to replace mere service with heartfelt love responses to God! The necessary work will not go undone, but the lives of God's people will be fulfilled rather than exhausted.

In His premiere initiation, Jesus met the issue of worship head on. He knew He was the Son of God, but He insisted that worship go to the entire Godhead. In this lengthy confrontation with Satan, Jesus also established a second vital principle of worship in declaring the exclusivity of worship. He was amazingly insightful when it came to worship.

6

Jesus' Insight

The story of the temptation of Jesus as told by both Matthew and Luke, and referred to by Mark, is more than an initiation into ministry. It was the time and place when Jesus developed principles of worship. He did not wait until He was in a public ministry before establishing a life of worship. He explored the principles of worship immediately after being proclaimed the Son of God. Worship is never the result of a ministry. It always flows out of a relationship. Once it was confirmed that Jesus was, indeed, the Son of God and that the Father was pleased with Him, worship principles began to form in Jesus.

Jesus' first worship experience was concerned far more with principle than with practice or passion. He was not in the heights of emotional frenzy, but in the wilderness being tempted by the devil. His emotions were directed more inward than outward, and He was fighting doubts more than He was feeling delights. His very person was being questioned, and His will was repeatedly assaulted. He was rapidly learning that worship is more faith than feeling; more a positional relationship than pleasant reveries.

From the very outset of His ministry, Jesus showed us by His example that until we deal positively with the substance of worship, we cannot safely deal with the sensations of worship. While it is true, as we have seen, that worship is the expression of a feeling we have for our Lord, the substance of worship is neither the feeling nor the expression of that feeling—it is the one Who inspired that feeling in the first place. Worship must deal with God first, last, and always.

Whenever the method of worship becomes more important than the person of worship, we have already prostituted our worship. Unfortunately, there are entire congregations who worship praise and praise worship, but who have not yet learned to praise and worship God in Jesus Christ. The song, the dance, the banners, and the shouting have been accepted as worship instead of being seen as means of expressing worship.

The Extent of Worship

It is impossible for us to measure the full extent of worship, for everyone worships something or someone at one time or another. Worship is a God-given instinct or drive almost as powerful as our sex drive. I have never read the journal of an explorer who claimed to have discovered a tribe of people anywhere on this earth who did not worship something.

Furthermore, I am unaware of any political or geographic division of persons in our modern world who do not worship.

Even the atheistic countries worship the state or the system, and often they worship their philosophy of life with a passion and dedication that would put many Christians to shame. Worship is not a choice; we must worship. We were made that way. Only the object of our worship remains our choice. Both Jesus and Satan knew this.

The issue, then, is not to find worshipers. Jesus did not tell the woman at Jacob's well that the Father was seeking worshipers. He told her that the Father was seeking those who worshiped Him. This has always been the problem—to find those who worship God exclusively.

Most Christians worship God occasionally and some do it only on Sundays, but few worship Him exclusively. Like the Philistines who added the captured Ark of God to their house of gods, many Christians merely add occasional worship of God to their lives that are already dedicated to position, power, possession, and poppycock. They painfully learn what the Philistines learned by the destruction of Dagon, their chief deity: if God remains, all other gods must go.

The Father searches for persons in whom His name, nature, attributes, and glory have constant attention—persons to whom nothing in life is more important than God Himself. Individuals whose minds automatically turn to God when not being used in conscious endeavors are the object of the Father's search.

"Fanaticism!" you say.

No. It is being in love. Do you remember in the weeks before your wedding, how your mind was constantly on your pledged marriage partner? You actually had to pry your mind free by a conscious effort in order to accomplish your work. This is what God desires. God is seeking persons who are so consciously in love with Him that every thought of their minds, every feeling of their emotions, and every response of their lives is in harmony with that love.

If God is Who He says He is, and if we are the believing people of God that we claim to be, then we must worship Him. This was the purpose of creation, and it is the reason for our redemption. God yearns for fellowship with His adoring children whose lives have been rescued from self-centeredness and restored to a God-consciousness. It is His desire, and it should be our delight. Jesus had this insight while He was still in the wilderness being tempted.

The Exploitation of Worship

The verse Jesus quoted when the devil tempted Him to divert His worship to Satan was a rather loose quote from Deuteronomy 6:13 (NKJV): "*You shall fear the LORD your God and serve Him . . . .*" There is no comma in the sentence, for "fear" and "serve" are seen as one action. The Hebrew word used here for "fear" is *yawray*, which means "to make afraid" or "to revere." The verse can be translated, "You shall revere the Lord your God," but Jesus substituted the word "worship" for "revere" as though the two were synonymous terms.

Who are we to argue with the Son of God Who from eternity to eternity is the object of heaven's worship? The book of Revelation, in picturing worship as it transpires in heaven, consistently shows reverence as the first step in worship. The great ones in the heavens bow before God, and redeemed men cast their crowns before the Lord, declaring that He is exclusively worthy to be worshiped.

How sad it is to see so many Christians who no longer think in terms of reverence and worship. They seek to approach God as though they were His equal or that God were their servant. Perhaps this lack of reverence indicates their doubt that God's presence is really among them. Even though losing the awareness of God in our midst is too terrible even to imagine, this loss of the awareness of God is far too common in our American churches. We modern Christians have learned a few principles of God and seem content to practice them without the presence of God.

Modern Christianity secularizes God to the point where we don't feel the need of the Divine presence. We secularize the gospel, we secularize evangelism, and we secularize our worship. We are devilishly clever in adapting the world's methods of doing business to the work of the kingdom.

We deliberately ignore all of Christ's warnings about the motivations and methods of the unconverted and function just like the person we are trying to convert. If the sound is turned down on the TV set, it is difficult to know what is being sold—records or Jesus. Pastors build their empires around themselves instead of on Jesus, and even a keen musician has a hard time telling the difference between the music of the church and that of the disco.

In many religious gatherings, the preaching of creativity has replaced the preaching of the Cross. Happiness, not holiness, has been set as the goal for the believer's life. We still talk about worship, but not the worship of God. Instead, people are led to worship a program, a doctrine, a denomination, a building, or a "feeling," but this is gross exploitation of worship as Jesus taught it. We now bring into our churches people who have no idea of what it means to love and worship God, because the sales route through which we brought them involved no personal encounter with God. We merely asked for a "united" sinner's prayer, handed them a Bible verse with a promise of forgiveness, and added their names to the church roll.

We sidestepped sin and crises. We didn't require repentance, restitution, or reform. It is little wonder, then, that so little true worship of God is to be found in our churches. If people have never met God, how can we expect them to worship Him?

The Exclusivity Of Worship

Perhaps our text is best translated, "You shall worship the Lord your God and Him only . . . . " All spiritual worship must have God as its object. Each local church exists to do corporately what individual Christian believers are called to do: worship God! This is our exclusive calling, and everything else in our lives must flow out of that worship.

If the purpose of our gathering together is to worship, then nothing should be allowed in the service that calls attention away from God. Any music that does not exalt God and draw us closer to Him should be considered out of place. Any individual who directs our attention to himself rather than to God is asking for adulation that belongs to God alone. Worship is one thing that God refuses to share with another, and those who seek to be worshiped will find a similar treatment as given to Lucifer: GET OUT!

Because worship is the mission of the Church, all satanic temptation is ultimately directed against worship. If Satan cannot get us to worship him directly, he will seek to divert or pervert our worship, and he is a master at this. In the heavens, he tempted the angels under his command to worship him instead of God. Those angels were cast down with Lucifer.

In Eden, Satan tempted Adam and Eve to eat of the forbidden fruit by telling them that when they ate it, they would know what God knew—good and evil—and therefore would be equal with God, so they could actually worship themselves. Humanism had an earlier beginning than most of us realize. As a result of submitting to this temptation, Adam and Eve were forever cast out of the Garden of Eden.

During the forty days of harassment in the wilderness, the devil dared to approach Jesus with the same temptation he had used so successfully with his angels in heaven: "Worship me!" Christ was offered the world without the pain and ignominy of the Cross in exchange for a shift in the object of worship. Jesus resisted it totally, and for the first time recorded in the Scriptures, the tempter was foiled in his attempt to divert worship away from Father God.

Jesus knew far better than we that all worship belongs to God. The Bible does not merely call believers to worship; it consistently tells us to "Worship God!" The object of our worship is far more important than the expression of our worship. If our minds and hearts are fixed upon God, our emotions and our spirits will find proper expression in response to God, but if our minds are fixed on anything other than God, no form of expression will be acceptable worship to God.

Expediency And Worship

The tempter did not cease his work after Jesus so successfully frustrated him in the wilderness. Throughout the ages he has continually tempted the Church to worship that which is beneath God Himself. Although the Bible promises that *"The Lord knoweth how to deliver the godly out of temptations"* (2 Peter 2:9, KJV), it would seem that many of the godly prefer the temptation to the deliverance. As it has so often been said, many Christians when faced with temptation say, "Get thee behind me, Satan and push!"

Just as in days gone by, the devil is busy in the Church today, tempting us to dispossess God. This was his goal in heaven, and it is still his goal here on earth. To accomplish his task, he needs the help of the Church, so he comes to its leadership with temptations such as holding firmly to the tradition of the elders no matter what God is presently revealing.

By the grace of God, I minister in a wide variety of denominations and fellowships. From time to time, I find myself preaching on praise in one of the more historic churches. At the end of the message, I call upon the people to stand and praise the Lord and they do so. God's Word does not return void.

I recall an occasion when I was taken to lunch by the pastor of such a church and after we placed our orders, he expressed his deep appreciation for my teaching on praise.

"I've never seen it in the Bible so plainly as I saw it this morning. There is no mistaking it—we are called to praise the Lord!" he said. "But, Dr. Cornwall," he added, "it will never work in our church."

"What do you mean, it won't work?" I responded. "It worked this morning."

"Well, yes, but you were a bit overwhelming, weren't you? You commanded the people to praise, and they obeyed you."

"That's what the Bible tells us leaders to do—to bring the people to praise," I said.

"Well," he continued, "it worked this morning, but it won't work again. You see, in our 300-year history, we've never done it this way."

"Oh, I see," I said. "What you are telling me is that although you see praise as a clear command in the Word of God, the traditions of your church are more important to you than what God has said."

"I wouldn't put it quite that way," he hedged.

"But that is the way Jesus put it when He was here," I replied.

How sad it is to fall for that time-worn temptation to stay with the old and familiar even when the new emphasis is clearly commanded by God Himself. Tradition can be as serious a bondage as sin, and it need not be 300 years old to become a trap.

At other times, we are tempted to hold tenaciously to our preplanned program rather than set it aside for a move of the Spirit. There is nothing unspiritual about a program. Every service should have a program just in case God does not show up, but if the presence of the Lord seems to direct us in a way unlike our planned schedule, file the program away and go with God. After all, He knows better than we do how He would like to be worshiped at any given moment.

The enemy also entices us to exalt ourselves over God. We are tempted to bring America's humanism and "rights" into our relationship with God and the Church. We fail to remember that when we allowed God to run the awl through our ear and place a golden earring in the hole to keep it from healing up, we became a love-slave with no rights whatsoever. God reigns—we do not!

Another temptation the devil brings against believers is that of adoring someone beneath God—worshiping a position or one in a position. Christians sometimes bow to power or to the powerful person and venerate prestige. We all need our heroes, and while we resist worshiping sports heroes or entertainment figures the way the world does, we unduly honor and praise some of the Christian leaders who are very much in the public eye. This is very pleasing to the devil, for as long as we are adoring someone beneath God, we will not be extolling God in worship, and that is the purpose of Satan's temptation.

All temptation is concerned with worship. If Satan cannot get us to worship him, he will try to prevent us from worshiping God. All too often the temptation is successful. If we are going to enter into a fruitful ministry in these days, we must follow the pattern of Jesus and refuse to worship anyone and anything other than God Himself. Purity in worship will produce purity in lives and service.

Jesus had the insight to settled the issue of the object of His worship before He ever entered into His ministry. So must we. Once Jesus settled this issue, He gloriously entered into the product of worship that God Himself provides: victory! Jesus became invincible.

7

Jesus Invincible

It was not by accident that Jesus met the devil the very first time He faced the issue of personal worship, for the devil is vitally concerned with worship. The book of Revelation lists four special offices that Satan fills. He is called "tempter, persecutor, accuser, and deceiver." These are more than mere titles. These are job descriptions.

Before his fall he was called "Lucifer," but after he and his angels were cast out of heaven, that name was never again applied to him. Instead, he is called the devil, Satan, and the serpent. The word "devil" comes from the Greek word *diabolus*, meaning "false accuser." The name "Satan" comes from the Greek word *satanos*, which means "true accuser," and the story of the serpent in the Garden of Eden lets us know why he is called "serpent."

His special power is deception through accusation and temptation. He accuses us to God, he indicts God to us, and he denounces us to ourselves. In order to prevent or pervert our worship, he must discredit all that God is, everything God has said, and what we have become in Christ Jesus.

During the forty days when he was granted permission to test Jesus, he unleashed every spiritual energy he could summon. The few words recorded in Matthew's account of this temptation are, at best, but a summary of what was said. Day and night the accuser challenged what Christ believed about Himself, what His cousin John had declared, and what God had said from heaven. It was all-out mental warfare and Jesus won! He proved to be invincible.

Jesus used the Word of God to gain victory over the tempter. I doubt if Jesus quoted Scripture verses in order to scare the devil. Since the devil rebelled against the Living Word Himself, it is hard to believe that he would be very terrified at anything God wrote. It is far more likely that Jesus quoted these verses for Himself.

When the devil assailed Jesus with accusations and tempting programs, Jesus cried out to know the will of the Father, for He always did the Father's will. During this season, He was not only isolated from other people—He was actually cut off from God.

Driven inward by the constant tirades of the devil, Jesus sought some clue to God's will in the matter. From deep within His spirit came Scripture passages that He had learned as a boy in the village synagogue. His spirit joyfully responded, "This is My Father's will." Quoting these verses out loud merely reinforced His decision to do things His Father's way, and it let the devil know that God's will, not Satan's, would be done.

Worship Resists the Devil

Once it was completely established that Jesus would do only the will of His Father, the temptation ended: *"Then the devil left Him"* is Matthew's report (Matthew 4:11, NKJV). It has always been this way. We can victoriously resist the devil when we are steadfast in our worship of God. The Word has always been invincible, and John declared Jesus to be the Word incarnate (John 1:1). The New Testament teaches us, *"Therefore submit to God. Resist the devil and he will flee from you"* (James 4:7, NKJV). The quoting of Bible verses does not drive off the enemy. He is driven away by the application of those verses to the areas of our lives that are being assaulted by this enemy of God. The real conflict has always been between the will of God and the will of Satan.

As long as we insist upon functioning in our own wills, we will repeatedly be assaulted by the enemy who seeks to align our wills with his desire to override the will of God. Once our will is completely submitted to God's will, the devil has no further power over us in that area.

From time to time, I have had persons ask me to lay my hands on them and pray for them. They stated that there was an area in their lives that the enemy had tempted successfully again and again. "I want you to pray that God will give me complete victory over this temptation," they would say.

"But God has given you the victory," I would respond. "What you are telling me is that you have refused to obey the Word of God in this area of your life, and the enemy has successfully tripped you up again and again. You don't need my prayer; you need to obey God's Word. Once that decision has been made, the tempter will leave you alone."

Perhaps you have walked the midway section of the county fair or have attended a carnival in your area and have seen a man with a portable table on which were three walnut shells. He would put a small white ball under one shell and begin to move the three shells around, all the time telling you to keep your eye on the shell with the white ball under it. He invited you to bet your money that you could tell him where the white ball was when he stopped the shuffle. If there is no greed in you, there is no way he can draw you into his game, but if you feel that you have a right to something you have not earned, you may very well pour your whole week's paycheck into betting against this man's slight of hand.

Similarly, if there is no rebellion against the will of God, the devil has no basis for temptation in the life of a believer. Jesus later told His disciples, ". . . *the prince of this world is coming. He has no hold on me*" (John 14:30). Jesus had so set His will to do the Father's will that there was nothing in Him upon which the enemy could draw. Jesus was invincible!

The safest answer to the demonic is the divine. Our submission to God becomes a resistance to the devil. Our immunity to satanic interference is proportional to our submission to Jesus Christ.

It is likely that we will be more aware of demonic interference and accusation when we prepare to pray and worship than at any other time. I have heard multiple testimonies that match my own experience. As I begin to approach God through thanksgiving and praise, my mind fills with past failures and recent unrighteous actions. Since I have only begun to draw near to God, and I know that He doesn't speak until I am in His presence, I am assured that this is not God dealing with me. Besides, He deals in love, not in accusation.

My second check is to determine whether the thoughts are originating within me or are being projected from another source. I have an accusing heart that can sidetrack me from worshiping God, but on this occasion, I am aware that the thoughts are being projected from outside of me, and I recognize this to be demonic activity. If I begin to deal with this by rebuking, taking authority, casting out, or even trying to reason with it, the enemy will have succeeded in preventing me from worshiping God. All my time, energy, and attention will have been focused on the devil instead of on God.

Over the years I have learned that in such circumstances it is better to ignore the taunts of the satanic and to deal exclusively with God's Word and His Spirit. Even though the accusations may be true, they have been answered in the blood of Jesus, and I stand approved in the presence of God the Father. I fear that we Christians waste a lot of spiritual energy fighting battles that have already been won at Calvary. Rejoicing in Jesus is better than rebuking Satan, for once we settle the issue of Whom we will worship, the devil will leave us.

Worshipers have the most consistently victorious lives, for they have developed a heart fixation on God that cannot be disturbed by temptation or tribulation. They can accept negative circumstances without letting them affect their relationship with God. They have learned to submit their will to God and to express their love to Him through Jesus, and nothing with which the enemy can assail them affects their love relationship with Jesus.

Worship Enlists Divine Ministries

The same verse that assures us, *"Then the devil left Him,"* also informs us, *"And behold, angels came and ministered to Him"* (Matthew 4:11, NKJV). Please remember that this temptation covered forty days and forty nights during which Jesus neither ate, slept, nor had fellowship with another person or with God. The constant spiritual pressure exhausted Him in body, soul, and spirit. He was drained physically, emotionally, and spiritually.

When it was over, He did not come crawling out of the wilderness in a weak or emaciated condition, nor was He begging for help. Jesus walked out in the power and anointing of the Spirit to launch a ministry that no man on this earth has yet equaled.

How could He experience such devastating onslaughts of spiritual forces for so long a period and still come out victorious and powerful in God? He could, and did, because when the devil was through taking from Him, the angels of God came and ministered to Him. Anything that Satan may have diminished, the angels replenished.

It is as true for today's sons of God as it was true then for the Son of God. Worshipers have access to divine strength about which non-worshipers know nothing. God still commissions His angels to bring us every needed strength.

Speaking of angels, the Bible asks, *"Are not all angels ministering spirits sent to serve those who will inherit salvation?"* (Hebrews 1:14). So much of the work of God in the Old Testament was done through the ministry of angels. Shouldn't we expect it to be just as true in New Testament times? God doesn't change. Neither does human need.

True worship can occur only in the presence of God. We may praise from a distance, but we worship only when we are near God. But Who is the God we worship? Stepping aside from all philosophical and theological arguments, the New Testament gives us four foundational definitions of God:*"God is love"* (1 John 4:16), *"God is light"* (1 John 1:5), *"I am holy"* (1 Peter 1:16), and *"Our God is a consuming fire"* (Hebrews 12:29).

These four definitions of God are the four major sources of energy used on this earth. *Light* (the sun) is the major source of natural energy known to man. *Love* is the strongest emotional energy in this world. *Holiness* is the source of all spiritual energy in this world, and none of us would deny that

70

fire is energy. It is a force that converts energy from a solid source into a flame that produces light and heat.

God is the root source of natural energy, emotional energy, spiritual energy, and the conversion of energy from one form to another. When we stand in the presence of God in worship, we stand in the midst of all this energy. No wonder, then, that just like Jesus, we can be invincible over the power of the enemy. With God before us, His Spirit within us, and His angels around us, how could we keep from being renewed during the seasons of worship?

Worshiping saints are *"strengthened with might through His Spirit in the inner man"* (Ephesians 3:16, NKJV), just as Paul prayed for the saints in Colossae that they might be *"strengthened with all might, according to His glorious power"* (Colossians 1:11, NKJV).

Throughout the years, the saints who have accomplished the most in the kingdom of God have been great worshipers. Men who spent two, three, or more hours a day in the presence of God in prayerful worship moved mountains for God. They found a source of spiritual energy that today's Church must locate in order to survive the days before us.

Since *"our struggle is not against flesh and blood, but against the rulers, against the authorities, against the powers of this dark world and against the spiritual forces of evil in the heavenly realms"* (Ephesians 6:12), we need a source of spiritual energy that exceeds mental preparedness, soulish excitement, and physical discipline. We need the power and might of God, and this is available from the presence of God.

Worshipers stand in His presence and enjoy His person while unconsciously absorbing spiritual energy from Him. This energy is a by-product of our worship, but it is a necessary product for our lives on earth. It is what made Jesus invincible, and it will make us victorious as well.

Worship Expresses Our Reason for Living

Jesus had searched for His purpose of being and was assured that He was the Son of God. Then He was immediately tested or tempted in the matter of worship, for Satan knew that if Jesus entered into worship, He would not only reinforce His purpose of being, but would find a glorious expression of the purpose.

Worship helps us find who we are in God and why He has placed us here on the earth. Having been made in God's image, we have within us the capacity to know God and the instinct to worship Him. The worship of God releases this capacity and instinct. Worship fulfills our reason for being.

God's highest desire is that every one of His believing children should so love and adore Him that they are continuously in His presence in spirit and in truth—pure worship. Actually, worship becomes a completely personal love experience between God and the worshiper, and this should be continuous. There is no limit to what God can do through us if we are His yielded and purified people—worshiping and showing forth His glory and His faithfulness.

In handling Satan's temptation, Jesus established that we should worship God only, and that spiritual service and divine energy will come out of that worship. There can be no human substitute for this kind of worship and Spirit-given response to God, Who is our Creator, Redeemer, and Lord.

We have no choice but to worship, for it is a created instinct within each of us. Our only choice is in the object and manner of our worship, and there Jesus gave us some specific guidelines. He came on the scene as the divine instructor.

8

Jesus' Instruction

From the wilderness of temptation, Matthew quickly shifted his attention to a hillside in the Galilee area. Jesus' early ministry of teaching, preaching, and healing the sick drew needy people to Him. Matthew records: *"Large crowds from Galilee, the Decapolis, Jerusalem, Judea and the region across the Jordan followed him. Now when he saw the crowds, he went up on a mountainside and sat down. His disciples came to him, and he began to teach them"* (Matthew 4:25; 5:1-2).

What followed is often called the "Sermon on the Mount." It is a masterpiece that deals most succinctly with the principles for Christian living. Far from being a parody of the Law, it is a series of proclamations that get right to the heart of individual living and the everyday issues each of us faces.

These teachings of Jesus frequently cut across the grain of the religious teaching of that time by offering a series of choices rather than the harsh declarations the Jewish teachers imposed upon the people. Jesus consciously sidestepped the religious thought of His day and heralded the challenge of His Old Testament namesake, *"Choose for yourselves this day whom you will serve"* (Joshua 24:15).

Having successfully defeated the devil in the matter of worship, Jesus began to teach principles that govern our approach to God. Before He taught specifically on worship, Jesus taught on vertical and horizontal relationships, for He knew far better than we do that worship is but an expression of a correct relationship with God.

While He did not address some factors that are common to worship, the section of the sermon that particularly deals with choices has the *Lord's Prayer* in the very middle of it. It doesn't take great insight to realize that these choices affect our approach to God. Worship is the result of a series of choices, for the will, not the emotions, determines our worship. The choice we have in worship is never *if* we will worship, but *whom* we will worship. Once we have determined to be a worshiper of God, we are faced with a series of choices that will vitally affect that worship. These are choices that determine our attitude far more than other actions.

Jesus never spoke about choices in how to express our worship; He was more concerned with how we form that worship in our spirit. Some groups today are almost militant over the method of expression they have espoused, but Jesus was militant about the *attitude* of the worshiper, for worship must always come from an inner point of view. Worship involves a number of factors, including the mental, spiritual, and emotional. None of us will worship with the same degree of wonder and love at all times, but the attitude and the state of mind must remain consistent with God's Word if we are worshiping the Lord.

Jesus' greatest contribution to the doctrine of worship was His continual assurance that God's worshiping people will be a purified people; a people delighting in the spiritual disciplines of a life pleasing to God. He taught us that the eternal plan was not to bring God down to our level so that we could worship Him, but to take humanity up to God through Him.

The first hint of our being able to ascend into God's presence as worshipers comes in the pattern for prayer that Jesus gave about midway through His Sermon on the Mount. He taught the people that they, the humble peasants under the dictatorship of Rome, could pray, "*Our Father*." Because God had become man, mankind could relate to God as their heavenly Father. How quickly this changed basic attitudes toward worship. Worship became far more intimate and personal, and all actions in worship would have to be governed by the attitudes of the worshiper toward the One being worshiped.

Surrounding this prayer pattern, Jesus wove a tapestry of positive and negative attitudes that would seriously affect any attempt to approach God. The choice the listeners made would determine the character of their worship. The alternatives listed in the sixth chapter of Matthew can be summarized into four categories: *choice of audience, forgiveness, masters, and trust.*

Choice Of Audience

The first is a choice of the audience a person wants for his or her worship. Jesus offered the choice of doing charitable deeds publicly, accompanied by the sound of a trumpet to call attention to oneself, or doing them so secretly as to "*not let your left hand know what your right hand is doing*" (Matthew 6:3, NKJV).

Jesus offered a choice between the long public prayers of the hypocrites or the secret prayer of a worshiper. He also offered a choice of audience when fasting. He said, "*When you fast, do not look somber as the hypocrites do, for they disfigure their faces to show men they are fasting. I tell you the truth, they have received their reward in full. But when you fast, put oil on your head and wash your face, so that it will not be obvious to men that you are fasting, but only to your Father, who is unseen; and your Father, who sees what is done in secret, will reward you"* (Matthew 6:16-18).

The decision Jesus placed before us was whether our religious performance, prayer, and piety were to be played before an audience of people or done completely unto God. The choice will determine whether that worship is offered to God or actually offered to the people of God with God's name on it.

We all know a variety of persons who will do good only if their action will, in turn, be good to their public image. We've heard more than our share of lengthy public "sermon prayers" that by their very nature prove there is little, if any, private praying in that person's life. Similarly, there are people who feel they must publicly display their piety whether by dress, sad countenance, pious speech, or demonstrable religious actions. The common denominator among these worshipers is that they want to be seen. They are self-conscious, not God-conscious, and whether or not they realize it, they are worshipers of self rather than of the living God. Their worship motives are impure, but Jesus said that they receive their reward from men who compliment them and tell them how great they are in God's kingdom.

True worshipers don't care what people think of their worship. Everything they do is unto the Love of their souls, and His approval is all that matters to them. Singers, dancers, banner-wavers, and worship leaders must make this decision in every public service—for which audience do I want to play—God or the people?

Perhaps this choice could be reduced to the choice between pride and humility. We must constantly remind ourselves that the proud and lofty man or woman cannot worship God in spirit and truth.

Choice of Forgiveness

The second major choice Jesus the great instructor laid before us concerns forgiveness. Immediately following the Lord's Prayer,

Jesus said, *"For if you forgive men when they sin against you, your heavenly Father will also forgive you. But if you do not forgive men their sins, your Father will not forgive your sins"* (Matthew 6:14-15).

Jesus clearly stated that our attitudes toward one another affect our attitudes toward God, and worse than that, control God's attitude toward us. While mere religion may allow an escape from daily life, worship brings our daily life to God as a consecration to the divine will. When we worship, we bring all that we are to God. If we have an unforgiving spirit toward another person, we bring that spirit into the presence of God. During worship, we ask God for forgiveness, but He says, "I will, if you *will*."

Earlier in this sermon Jesus had told the multitude, *"Therefore, if you are offering your gift at the altar and there remember that your brother has something against you, leave your gift there in front of the altar. First go and be reconciled to your brother; then come and offer your gift"* (Matthew 5:23-24).

The protective barrier we build around ourselves to keep others from getting in to hurt us also keeps us from getting out to love either them or God. Jesus said that it was inefficient to continue in religious exercises when we realize that nothing is getting out of our heart. "Tear down the wall. Get back into a harmonious relationship with your brother" was Christ's solution to an unresponsive heart during times of worship.

On a few occasions, before I could enter into an anointing to preach, I have had to leave the pulpit and go down to my wife in the congregation to ask her forgiveness for an action or attitude that had built a barrier between us. Nothing can bring us face to face with our inner attitudes more quickly than entering into worship. At times it seems that God is like a gigantic mirror that reflects the flaws in our lives, but this revelation is for restoration, not devastation. God wants us to actively change what we can change, which then frees Him to effect in us those changes we are unable to make.

Jesus said that we are to forgive in order to be forgiven, and that we should forgive because we have been forgiven. When Peter came to the Lord, quite proud of his willingness to forgive a sinning brother up to seven times, *"Jesus answered, 'I tell you, not seven times, but seventy-seven times'"* (Matthew 18:22). If we think of our relationships with others as occupying about twelve hours of each day, Jesus was suggesting that if a brother sinned against us every fifteen minutes of the day, we should be prepared to forgive him each time.

To explain why, Jesus told the parable of the king who tried to collect what was due him from his servants. One servant was deeply in debt to the king and pleaded for mercy, and the king forgave him the debt. This servant went out to collect a very small sum owed him by another servant, and instead of showing mercy when the man could not pay the debt, he sent him to prison. When the king heard of this, he revoked his generosity and had that first servant delivered to the jailers *"until he should pay back all he owed"* (Matthew 18:34).

Jesus was simply saying that if we would be true worshipers of the Father, we cannot expect grace for ourselves while showing a lack of mercy to others. What we receive, we are expected to give. Forgiveness to us must be followed by forgiveness by us if we would be partakers of the divine image that makes worship so valid.

All the grace of God we have received flows back to God as worship. Faith, love, obedience, forgiveness—all of these strive in us to worship God. If there is anything within us that refuses to worship, there is nothing within us, then, that worships God very well.

Choice of Masters

Paul's searching question: *"Don't you know that when you offer yourselves to someone to obey him as slaves, you are slaves to the one whom you obey whether you are slaves to sin, which leads to death, or to obedience, which leads to righteousness?"* (Romans 6:16), could well be a paraphrase of Jesus' statement, *"No one can serve two masters. Either he will hate the one and love the other, or he will be devoted to the one and despise the other. You cannot serve both God and Money"* (Matthew 6:24). Whether we like it or not, when we choose our *master*, we automatically select our way of life.

The seeking of wealth and the securing of things are contrary to worship, for worship is an expression of dependence upon God, while amassing treasures on earth is a declaration of independence. The passion for possessions becomes a controlling obsession that limits a person's vision to the temporal. Jesus said, *"Where your treasure is, there your heart will be also"* (Matthew 6:21). He also spoke of the controlling power of our eye, suggesting that what we look at will determine our value systems.

Because this is such a controlling force in most of our lives, Jesus dealt with it extensively; trying to get us to see that life is far more than food, clothing, and where we live. He pointed to the birds of the air and the grass of the field; showing the beauty and glory God bestows on them. He then asked the question: *"If that is how God clothes the grass of the field, which is here today and tomorrow is thrown into the fire, will he not much more clothe you, O you of little faith?"* (Matthew 6:30).

Some have interpreted this passage as Jesus' condemnation against wealth and possessions. They felt that poverty is holiness and wealth is unholy, but Jesus never taught that money is sin—it is the *"love of money"* that is so destructive to believers. It is one's attitude, not one's accumulation, that helps or hinders his or her worship.

The American society has taught us to love things and use people to get them, but Jesus taught us to love people and use things to bless them. When we make this change in our attitude, it is God's pleasure to pour through our hands many things with which we can bless others.

When Jesus was undergoing temptation, Satan said to Him, *"'All this I will give you,' he said, 'if you will bow down and worship me'"* (Matthew 4:9). This is still a powerful temptation—to focus on things as a reward for worship—but we forget that it is a reward only for worshipers of *"the ruler of this world."* In contrast to this, Jesus said, *"For the pagans run after all these things, and your heavenly Father knows that you need them. But seek first his kingdom and his righteousness, and all these things will be given to you as well"* (Matthew 6:32-33). In both verses, "things" are available. In Matthew 4:9, they are given as a reward. In Matthew 6:32-33, they are added as a necessary by-product for life. In the first, "things" become the master; in the second, the Father is the Master.

He who worships money and possessions has a temporal god who cannot enter heaven, cannot bring happiness on earth, and is a disillusionment to all who serve him. That god is a severe taskmaster who can never say, "That's enough," nor has he ever been heard to say, "Well done, good and faithful servant."

Jesus did not say that the person who trusts in riches could not enter the kingdom of God, but He did say that it would be as difficult as leading a camel through the eye of a needle—or, in modern parlance, about as hard as driving a Mercedes through a revolving door.

Choice of Trust

While discussing the issue of which master worshipers would serve, Jesus raised the issue of who would be the object of our *trust*. Anxiety about necessary provisions in life and worry about our future are two negative influences upon our worship.

I realize we live in a culture very different from the one in which Jesus lived, and I am aware that anxiety and worry have become a part of our nature here in America, but Jesus was teaching the principle of dependence upon the Father rather than dependence upon self as a basis for living.

In the past fifteen years I have encountered pastor after pastor who refused to move under the direction of the Holy Spirit because of the three P's in their lives: parsonage, paycheck, and pension. They feared that if they stepped out to serve God directly, their church organization would strip them of their security and they would have no way to care for themselves. "In our denomination we trust" should be inscribed on their money.

Their sin is no greater than ours when we fret, worry, fuss, and spend sleepless nights over our futures. Either God is in charge of our lives or He is not. If He is, what is there to worry about? If He is not, why not? Have we withdrawn the control of our lives from His Fatherly hands?

We cannot be both anxious and trustful. If we are worshipers, we should give God control of our lives as well as offering Him compliments. Since worship is two lovers responding to one another, shouldn't our level of trust in God at least equal the trust the young lady has in the object of her affections? If God can be trusted with our emotions and our eternal destiny, it is self-evident that He can be trusted with our temporal life for the few moments we are here on earth.

Worshipers trade anxiety for trust. They have found that God deals with His children with love, He is always more than fair, and His provisions are excessively sufficient. Like the children of Israel, who had manna and water even on the days they were in open rebellion against God, worshipers learn that God's provision for their lives is due to His love for them far more than because of their love for Him.

If the right choices are made regarding to which audience we will play, whether we are willing to forgive, which master we will serve, and in whom we will trust, we are prepared inwardly to become true worshipers of God. These choices test the quality of the worshiper. In Christ's major discourse on worship later in His ministry, He gave us a criterion by which we could test the quality of our worship. We don't have to guess. We can know if

81

our worship is correct, for Jesus gives us the ground rules by which we will be inspected.

9

Jesus' Inspection

The Bureau of Weights and Measures was established very early in the organization of our nation's government. Standard measures for time, distance, volume, and weight were set up. A pound is exactly the same all across America because it must meet the standard set by this Bureau. Personal opinion does not establish the volume of a gallon—there is a standard that must be met. There are inspectors who test and check various products to assure the pubic that these standards are being adhered to.

What is true nationally is true corporately and individually. No manufacturer or service organization would remain in business very long without a quality control program. Before the item or service is made available to the public, there must be inspectors who determine whether the product meets the necessary preset standards. This inspection cannot be based on impression, inclination, or influence. It must follow guidelines that are known to the persons who produce the product or service. The purpose of the inspection is to assure the end user that the product is what it is supposed to be.

Jesus dared to set Himself up as the inspector of worship. He, alone, knows what is acceptable to God and what is not. He looks beyond the way worship looks and sounds, and checks the motivation, the direction, and the sincerity of our worship. Even after His ascension into heaven, He remains anxious that the worship ascending to the Father has the correct fragrance. We read: *"Another angel, who had a golden censer, came and stood at the altar. He was given much incense to offer, with the prayers of all the saints, on the golden altar before the throne. The smoke of the incense, together with the prayers of the saints, went up before God from the angel's hand"* (Revelation 8:3-4). Jesus mixes the true fragrance of heaven's worship with the insipid incense that ascends from earth, so that when it reaches the throne of God, its fragrance is accepted as true worship.

The compassionate ministry of Jesus took Him into the region of Judea near the Dead Sea, where so many people responded to Him that the Pharisees became alarmed that He baptized more disciples than His cousin, John, did. Rather than deal with this religious jealousy, and being totally unmoved by being designated the number-one minister of His day, Jesus chose to return to the Galilean area with its beautiful Sea of Galilee.

The journey was, of course, on foot and it took Him through the land of Samaria. About midway in this journey, He gave in to His weariness and sat down by Jacob's well near Sychar, while His disciples went on into the city to purchase something to eat. While the disciples were gone, a woman from the city came to draw some water for household use, and Jesus asked her for a drink of water.

This simple request, very common in the East, produced a confrontation that induced confusion and ultimately led to her confession of her unclean marital status. That opened the way for Jesus to give His greatest recorded discourse on worship. I have dealt quite conclusively with this confrontation in my earlier book, *Let Us Worship*. The purpose of taking another look at it is to show that in discussing worship with this woman, Jesus gave us a standard, a gauge, or a touchstone by which to judge the genuineness or the quality of worship.

Jesus declared to this Samaritan woman, "*A time is coming and has now come when the true worshipers will worship the Father in spirit and truth, for they are the kind of worshipers the Father seeks*" (John 4:23). This is God's touchstone—His bureau of measurement—to determine the purity of worship.

It is unfortunate that the Church has been willing to allow individuals and sectarian groups to establish their own rules of authenticity for worship. Some measure it by its beauty, others by its volume, and some by its length. Jesus gave us three separate measurements by which to test the validity of any person's worship. He said that:

1. All worship must be directed to the Father.
2. True worship will be in man's spirit.
3. Pure worship will be offered in truth.

Today's Church could be spared much confusion and conflict if worship was judged by this divine standard rather than by the standard of what is popularly acceptable to the congregation.

The Benchmark of the Father

In making topographical surveys, a surveyor often puts a mark on a permanent object to serve as an elevation reference. He calls this the *benchmark*. This term has been adopted by others who aren't surveyors and is used for a point of reference for measurement.

Jesus clearly placed His Father as the benchmark of worship. Everything done in worship must measure up to this mark of the Father. The very first point of reference to be checked when seeking to determine the validity of any worship is the object of that worship. If God is not the obvious object, then that worship is false worship, no matter how beautiful, elaborate, or moving it may be.

While this may seem self-evident, it is disturbing to observe the vast amount of public worship that is directed to an object far lower than the benchmark of the Father. Some churches seem to worship "worship" rather than worship God, and others worship the emotion that worship gives them—they enjoy the spiritual high they get in worshiping together.

Other groups don't seem to even have a specific object for their worship; they merely call for a "time of worship," and each individual is allowed to focus his or her thoughts on whatever he or she desires. Of course, there are those groups whose adulation goes to the pastor rather than to God, but this is hero worship, not spiritual worship.

Sometime back, I was guest speaker in a church that was known for its worship. I stood on the platform observing the variety of worship expressions in the congregation during the Sunday morning service. They sang with enthusiasm, raised their hands on command, and some even took the liberty to do a little dance in the isle. Everything seemed to be done *"decently and in order"* as Paul had suggested in 1 Corinthians 14:40.

Unfortunately, something didn't seem right. I silently prayed, "Dear Lord, I can't find You in the service this morning. Is there something wrong with me that in the midst of this worship expression, I can't have an awareness of Your presence?"

I felt impressed in my spirit to take another look at the congregation. It was as though a cartoonist had drawn a balloon over each person's head, and in that balloon was written what was on the mind of the individual. One was thinking of his new car; another of a lover. A third was rejoicing in her home, and another was thinking of the football game to be played that afternoon. No one was thinking of God—each was lost in his or her own world of loves, desires, and ambitions. Their worship was not directed to Father God in heaven; they were worshiping idols here on earth. Their worship sounded and looked beautiful, but I was in a house of idolatry. It broke my heart and I wept almost uncontrollably. How grieved God must have been.

All worship that is not offered to God falls short of the benchmark of the standard Jesus set for true worship. No matter how beautiful the method or how pure the motive, unless God is the direct object of that worship, it is manifestly false worship—idolatry.

In declaring that the true worshipers will worship the Father, Jesus was not excluding Himself or the Holy Spirit from being the objects of our worship. After His season of temptation, Jesus was never in doubt about His divinity. He allowed people to worship Him, and He clearly admitted that He was the Son of God at His trial.

In speaking of Jesus, Paul wrote, *"He is the image of the invisible God, the firstborn over all creation . . . For God was pleased to have all his fullness dwell in him"* (Colossians 1:15, 19). Remember, Jesus came to give us a revelation of the Father.

It is likely that we can more comfortably approach the Father through the Son, for we have a visualization of Jesus, but our concept of God is often so nebulous as to prevent the full focusing of our thoughts on Him. Perhaps the best formula for approaching God in both worship and prayer is, *"Through him we both have access to the Father by one Spirit"* (Ephesians 2:18). It is through Jesus, by the Spirit, and unto the Father.

The benchmark of worship is the object, not the formula, of the worship. Jesus told the woman at the well, *"You Samaritans worship what you do not know; we worship what we do know, for salvation is from the Jews"* (John 4:22).

Remember, the woman was arguing the fine point of where to worship—on the mountain in Samaria or in the Temple in Jerusalem—but Jesus reduced the issue to knowing the Person to Whom worship is given. The standard has not changed in the ensuing years. The first test of our worship must be, "Do you know Whom you are worshiping?" It must be more than tagging God's name to our worship liturgy; it is actually knowing God and worshiping Him out of that knowledge.

When Paul addressed the Athenians, he *"stood up in the meeting of the Areopagus and said, 'Men of Athens! I see that in every way you are very religious. For as I walked around and looked carefully at your objects of worship, I even found an altar with this inscription: TO AN UNKNOWN GOD. Now what you worship as something unknown I am going to proclaim to you'"* (Acts 17:22-23).

Isn't it likely that we need a few modern Paul's to travel through our churches and introduce the congregations to the God to Whom they build their buildings and express their worship? If we don't know Him, what depth can there possibly be to our worship? Can we satisfactorily extol the unseen, magnify the unknown, or love the unrevealed?

The express purpose for the coming of Jesus was to reveal the Father to us. The more we know Jesus, the more we will know of the Father. Jesus could declare that *"the hour is coming, and now is"* because He came to bring us from the unknown god to the true and living God.

God is seeking worshipers who have received sufficient revelation of Him through Jesus and the Holy Spirit to be able to respond to Him both knowledgeably and emotionally. The Father seeks such worshipers, the Son gives sufficient revelation of the Father, and the Spirit channels the worship responses of those who offer such extravagant respect and devotion to the Godhead to enable their worship to be genuine. Wherever this operation of God-assisting worship is absent, we have good reason to question the genuineness of that worship. God's person as both the object of worship and an assistance to worship is the benchmark by which worship is judged.

The Touchstone of the Spirit

In the early days of silver mining in the West, an assayer's office had a "touchstone." This stone was used to validate true silver ore. God's touchstone to determine genuine worship is to validate the *source* of our worship. When Jesus said that true worshipers will worship the Father in spirit, He left it to us to determine if He meant the human spirit or the Holy Spirit. Qualified interpreters of the Scriptures sustain both views, and perhaps each concept is valid.

The translators of the *King James Version of the Bible*, as well as many other translators, have used a lowercase "s" to indicate their conviction that the thrust of the Greek language used by Jesus indicates that He was referring to the human spirit. If so, Jesus was declaring that the touchstone for testing worship is whether or not it comes from a person's spirit.

Lately, some authors have written about the soul-spirit of man. They usually divide the soul from the spirit by artificial definitions, assigning emotions and will to the soul, and conscience and God-awareness to the spirit. While this may be excellent for theological study, it is completely impractical for daily living, for man's soul cannot be separated from his spirit without killing his body. The Bible itself does not make a clear distinction between the two. Actually, the Old Testament interchanges the two words as though they were synonyms.

Leaving the finer division between the soul and spirit for exposition by others, let's accept the firm probability that Jesus used the word spirit in the Old Testament concept of the inner nature of man. This is the part of man that has a conscience, a God-consciousness, a will, emotions, and feelings. It is the nonbiological part of a person—that which sets humanity apart from and above the animal world.

True worshipers respond to God from something higher than instinct or physical passion. We have an intellect that can be inspired to a concept of God. We have a will that can determine that worship is going to be offered, regardless of how we feel. We have emotions that can express themselves to God worshipfully.

The psalmist, in speaking of man, wrote, "*You made him a little lower than the heavenly beings and crowned him with glory and honor. You made him ruler over the works of your hands; you put everything under his feet*" (Psalm 8:5-6). Surely such a high creature is capable of high-level response to his Maker.

Perhaps Jesus was saying that a touchstone of worship is that true worship must come from the inner person. The performance of mere outer rituals cannot be classified as worship unless it is a genuine expression of an inner feeling. It is the attitude of the heart, the predisposition of man's soul, and the yearning of his spirit that make worship alive enough to please God.

In his book, *Whatever Happened To Worship?*, A.W. Tozer wrote, "The very last thing God desires is to have shallow-minded and worldly Christians bragging on Him." God wants some depth in our worship. He desires some feeling expressed to Him. As vital as words are, God wants a person's spirit in those words if they are to worship Him. As beautiful as singing and instrumental music may be in a worship service, unless they are releasing the spirits of the musicians to God, they are but "*a resounding gong or a clanging cymbal*" (1 Corinthians 13:1).

There is too much spiritless worship occurring in our churches. The choir sings, the instrumentalists play, the soloists sing, and occasionally the dancers dance, but there is no spirit in it. It lacks even the natural enthusiasm that a ball game can generate. All the while this is going on, the congregation sits as spectators of this dry presentation and applauds its performers. We dare call this worship!

Where are the tears of joy, the shouts of jubilation, or even the "amens" of identification? No wonder God comes to church so seldom, and we shouldn't be amazed that so few sinners accept Jesus as their Savior. If the saints can't be enthusiastic enough about Jesus to worship Him from their inner nature, what is there to attract one who has never met our Lord?

Ignore the trappings, the expertise, the beauty, the polish, and even the dedication when testing the validity of worship. Jesus does! The touchstone is man's spirit. Does the worship come from the heart or from the head? Is it the release of inner attitudes or merely the performance of an outer ritual? If a person's soul-spirit is not released toward God, it is not true worship—according to the criterion given to us by Jesus.

David seemed to understand the need to respond to God with the inner person, for he wrote, *"Praise the LORD, O my soul; all my inmost being, praise his holy name. Praise the LORD, O my soul, and forget not all his benefits"* (Psalm 103:1-2). Perhaps this should be our early prayer when we prepare to worship. Command the inner nature to respond to God with thanksgiving, rejoicing, reverence, and adoration. This is true worship, and a guideline by which we will be inspected and judged.

The Acid Test of Truth

In the California gold fields, the assayers used acid to test the purity of gold hence the term "the acid test." Jesus uses the acid test of truth when inspecting our worship. He told the woman at the well, *"True worshipers will worship the Father in spirit and truth, for they are the kind of worshipers the Father seeks."* Then He added, *"God is spirit, and his worshipers must worship in spirit and in truth"* (John 4:23-24).

While it is true that Jesus called Himself the Truth, the translators have not capitalized the word truth in either verse 23 or verse 24. It is not likely that the reference is to Jesus any more

91

than the reference spirit refers to the Holy Spirit. (This does no violence to the obvious fact that all worship must have the action of the Holy Spirit and be offered to the Father through Jesus Christ.) It is just that this is not the proof text to use for that concept.

What Jesus was emphasizing here is that worship, which proceeds to the Father from man's spirit, must be truthful. Honesty in communicating with God is an absolute prerequisite for true worship. While this may seem to be *prima facie*, it apparently is not well understood by many worshipers, for if you listen carefully to worship responses (whether your own or those given by others), you will hear much exaggeration, overstatement, distortion, and out-and-out lying. Even some of the songs we sing as worship responses are more fantasy than fact.

It is not that we come into God's presence to consciously lie to Him, but we often approach God with a desire to tell Him what we think He wants to hear instead of what is honestly in our hearts. We've learned a variety of religious cliches that may once have expressed the feelings of someone somewhere, but they aren't even close to our present inner feelings. Still, we recite them because we feel that they are what God wants to hear. Have we failed to grasp what David paid so great a price to learn: "*Surely you desire truth in the inner parts*" (Psalm 51:6)?

Some years ago I knelt in the prayer room of the church where I was pastoring and began my Monday morning prayer time by saying, "Lord, You are wonderful. I love You more than life itself."

Inwardly the Spirit rebuked me and said, "You liar. You're mad at God."

That was truth. On the preceding day, I felt that God had been very unfair with me in some things that had happened in the Sunday morning service, and I was seething with anger. Caught off guard, I heard myself say, "You're right. I am angry with God, and for good reason." I then went on to explain the reason for my anger, and since I expected divine judgement to be poured out on me almost immediately, I aired all previous actions of God that had angered me.

When I had finished, the Spirit asked, "Is that all?"

"That's all I can think of right now," I answered rather meekly.

"Well, Judson," the Spirit said, "that's the most honest prayer you have prayed so far this year."

I discovered that God would rather have me explode at Him in anger if that is honestly what is in me, than to pretend to have loving thoughts and feelings for Him. As long as I covered my feelings, God could do nothing about them, but when I expressed them, I opened myself for forgiveness, healing, and an adjustment of attitude. Honesty of heart and transparency of life are necessary if we are to maintain a loving relationship with God.

Religion seems to offer us cloaks and masks behind which to hide, but Jesus dares us to come out from behind everything that would conceal the true us and come to Him in complete truth. Perhaps the main reason there is so little truth in worship is that so few have found sufficient freedom to deal with truth. *"To the Jews who had believed him, Jesus said, 'if you hold to my teaching, you are really my disciples. Then you will know the truth, and the truth will set you free'"* (John 8:31-32). We learn the truth by being around the truth. Attention to God's Word will free us to accept what God says about us and to repeat that back to God in times of worship.

Truth may come out sounding more crude than learned religious phrases, but Jesus said the acid test for pure worship is truth. God prefers a truthful expression, however crude it may sound, above the flowery prayer of an untrue heart.

Since worship is far more than a mind-set, Jesus taught us that expressions of worship must be directed to the Father from a person's spirit in a truthful manner. Because this takes conscious effort, we often need to be motivated to move beyond praise and enter into worship. Jesus has made Himself available to initiate that worship experience.

10

Jesus Initiator

The book of Hebrews urges us: "*Let us fix our eyes on Jesus, the author and perfecter of our faith*" (Hebrews 12:2). *The Berkeley Bible* translates it, "*. . . with our eyes on Jesus, the Cause and Completer of our faith,*" while *Montgomery* puts it, "*. . . the pioneer and perfecter of our faith.*" If, as I have projected, worship is far more an expression of our faith than a release of our feelings, Jesus is the beginning and end of our worship. He inspires it and He receives it. He creates the desire, and He fulfills that desire.

Immediately after the Father made a public declaration that Jesus was His Son, Jesus was driven of the Spirit into the wilderness to be tempted and tested. It was His initiation into ministry, and the heart of the testing concerned worship. He was not released into ministry until He came to grips with the importance and power of worship. It is unlikely that we will be initiated into ministry without a similar confrontation with the need to worship. The disciples weren't.

Although the disciples were hand picked by Jesus and spent days and nights with Him, they did not worship until Jesus instigated that worship through self-revelation. Peter, the extrovert, seems to have been the first to see that Jesus was, indeed, the Son of God, and it made a worshiper out of him.

Peter's confession of faith was such a turning point in the lives of the disciples that all three of the synoptic Gospels record the incident. Since the Gospels were written years after these events transpired, and since none of the Gospels were intended to give a chronological record of the life of Jesus, it is not surprising to see that each writer placed this event against a different contextual background.

Matthew told of Peter's great revelation right after Christ's teaching to the disciples about the doctrine of the Pharisees and the Sadducees. Mark, however, told the story right after Jesus had opened the eyes of a blind man who first saw men as trees, but who was able to see perfectly after a second touch by Jesus. Luke tied the incident to the story of Jesus feeding the five-thousand men with only five loaves of bread and two fish.

Any one of these incidents could well have prepared Peter for a fresh revelation, for no one ever taught with divine authority as Jesus did. Watching a blind man regain his sight in progressive stages may have inspired Peter to allow God to give him a second touch on his spiritual eyes. The miracle of feeding so vast a multitude of people with so little food may have so greatly increased his faith that God could speak something fresh and new to him.

The atmosphere that surrounds supernatural demonstrations—whether they be anointed, authoritative teaching, miracles of healing, or supernatural provision for physical needs—is a good atmosphere in which to receive higher revelations of God's nature. When we see God at work among those He loves, we realize that He is far greater than we had previously believed. Only a heart of unbelief could let a person leave such a demonstration of God's love and power with the same concept of God he or she had before arriving. Even a person who is spiritually blind should be able to sense that something wonderful is happening and leave with an increased sense of the greatness of God. This is the way Jesus initiates worship.

The Release of Worship

Since worship is a response to the presence of God, the basic prerequisite for worship is to get into God's presence. According to Matthew, while the disciples were walking with Jesus from one place of ministry to another, Jesus began to question them about Himself. *"'Who do people say the Son of Man is?' They replied, 'Some say John the Baptist; others say Elijah; and still others, Jeremiah or one of the prophets'"* (Matthew 16:13-14).

This is a brief summary of a conversation that may well have covered the better part of the morning. A simple journey had turned into a worship session, for although the disciples had no stained-glass windows, pipe organs, or robed choirs, they were in the presence of God incarnate, talking TO Jesus ABOUT Jesus. Who needs the trappings of religion when we have the presence of Jesus in our midst?

There are times when the beauty of our corporate worship in the church lifts our inner nature into the presence of God. But some of our most glorious worship experiences come in our day-to-day walk with the Lord when He has chosen to talk with us *in the way*. It is important that we do not allow ourselves to become so dependent upon aids to worship that we cannot worship without them. Any time we have an awareness of the presence of God, we should be prepared to worship Him, whether it be while driving down the road, flying in a plane, working around the house, or sitting in a pew at church.

Worship is the expression to God of our concept of Him. It is far more than meditating upon that thought, and it goes beyond discussing that concept with others. It becomes an act of worship when we tell God what we know and think about Him. Since worship involves saying back to God our concepts of His being, person, and attributes, it can be done any time we're in a communicative relationship with God. That is what the disciples were doing on this walk—they were telling Jesus what they and others thought about Him. The release of worship is just that simple.

Worship Releases the Worshiper

When Jesus changed the conversation from what others were saying about Him to *"'But what about you?' he asked. 'Who do you say I am?'"* (Matthew 16:15), something wonderful happened inside Peter. Divine revelation opened his spiritual eyes to see that Jesus was actually the Christ—the long-awaited Messiah. Worship responses are usually initiated when Jesus is seen as He really is. When a great revelation of God comes while we are in His presence, worship is the natural release of that inner experience.

This principle was repeatedly seen at work during the earthly ministry of Jesus. Event after event opened the eyes of individuals and groups of people to see beyond the carpenter's son. They worshiped at the level of their revelation as a release of their spiritual experiences.

We read that after the healing of the paralytic, *"This amazed everyone and they praised God, saying, 'We have never seen anything like this!'"* (Mark 2:12). Worship was the natural release of their awe and wonder. Similarly, when

Jesus stopped a funeral procession at Nain to raise a mother's only son from the dead, *"They were all filled with awe and praised God. 'A great prophet has appeared among us,' they said. 'God has come to help his people'"* (Luke 7:16). Seeing a corpse rise out of a casket at the command of Jesus had to produce some very intense emotions, and worship was the way those excited feelings were released. It was a great way to initiate worship.

Similarly, after Jesus walked on the water to the boat where the disciples were fighting a contrary wind, and even bade Peter to walk to Him on the water, *"those who were in the boat worshiped him, saying, 'Truly you are the Son of God'"* (Matthew 14:33). The demonstration of divine power gave all of these people a changed concept about Jesus, and worship was the way they chose to release themselves to the Son of God. Once again Jesus was the initiator of their worship. He motivated them to worship.

The same principle is seen in Mary at the tomb after Christ's resurrection. She could only weep when she mistook Jesus for the gardener, but she recognized Jesus at once when He spoke to her. Her immediate response was to worship Him.

Peter was no exception. *"You are the Christ, the Son of the living God,"* he said (Matthew 16:16). Whether he whispered it or shouted it does not matter, for the measure of the revelation will determine the depth of the worship, but not the nature of the response.

The moment Peter said out loud to Jesus what God had inspired in his heart, he experienced a release that was life-giving. He had known many hours of talking with Jesus until, at times, it seemed that their minds almost touched each other. He had never experienced the joy, the inner peace, and the oneness with God that he did that day when his spirit touched Christ's Spirit in a moment of inspired worship. It was a glorious release.

All of us have a sense of being locked up in our earthly bodies, and at times the spirit within us screams for release, however momentary it may be. Some people in desperation turn to alcohol and various drugs as a way of release, and others seek release in sex or recreation. Rarely do they realize that they are trying to answer a cry of their spirits by feeding an appetite of their bodies. They are never successful in attaining a release—they only increase their bondage.

In worshiping, our spirits are released to touch the Spirit of God in a liberating way. Paul said, *"The Spirit himself testifies with our spirit that we are God's children"* (Romans 8:16). Confirmation and consolation are ours when our spirits actually contact the Spirit of God in worship. There are times of worship when our spirits are so dominant and so in touch with God's Spirit that it seems we may be having an out-of-body experience. Jesus is initiating worship. Speaking of himself, Paul wrote, *"I know that this man—whether in the body or apart from the body I do not know, but God knows was caught up to paradise. He heard inexpressible things, things that man is not permitted to tell"* (2 Corinthians 12:3-4). Spiritual ecstasy will do that to us. We touch new dimensions, we reach new heights of joy, and our spirits are so uninhibited that it does not seem possible that we are still in our bodies on this earth. The early Pentecostals used to refer to this as "having a little heaven to go to heaven in."

Worship not only releases the worshiper's spirit, but it also becomes a channel of release for his soul. Long pent-up emotions can comfortably be released in the presence of the Lord, for tears, sighs, shouts, songs, and even silence are all equally acceptable in worship. There are few other places in life that offer us this liberty.

In *Whatever Happened To Worship?*, A.W. Tozer commented, "If the Holy Spirit should come again upon us as in earlier times, visiting church congregations with the sweet but fiery breath of Pentecost, we would be greater Christians and holier soldiers. Beyond that, we would also be greater poets and greater artists and greater lovers of God and His universe."

In my own personal experiences and observations, I have decided that we Christians are often so highly charged emotionally from the pressures of life that we are resistant to the Holy Spirit. Just as a buildup of static electricity needs to be expended through grounding before the operator dares touch his computer, we need to expend this emotional energy before our inner man can get calm enough to really commune with God. Worship is the best grounding God has made available to us. It brings us into sync with Him in a pleasant and meaningful manner.

Worship Also Releases Jesus

When Peter gave full expression to his fresh revelation of just Who Jesus actually was, it seems that Jesus was almost as excited as Peter, for "*Jesus replied, 'Blessed are you, Simon son of Jonah, for this was not revealed to you by man, but by my Father in heaven'*" (Matthew 16:17).

Why was Jesus so animated at Peter's confession when this confession had been made several times already? The angels had declared Him to be the Messiah when He was born. At His circumcision, Simon had divulged that this was God's Christ. At His baptism, God had advertised that this was the Son of God incarnate. When Jesus confronted the demon-possessed man, the demons that inhabited this man "*shouted at the top of his voice, 'What do you want with me, Jesus, Son of the Most High God?'*" (Mark 5:7).

Until this time, the confession had come from angels, a prophet, God the Father, and demons, but now it came from one of His disciples. This released Jesus to function as the

Messiah among them. The great cry in the heart of God has always been to be what He actually is in the lives of those He loves, but our unbelief and our lack of praise and worship restrict Him from a full manifestation. When we worship God for a specific facet of His nature, we release Him to be that very thing in our lives.

Few of us realize how important praise and worship are in releasing God to function in our lives, although we are very aware of this principle in operation in everyday life. If our automobile malfunctions, we may ask friends to recommend a mechanic. When we get to the garage and specifically ask for that mechanic, we praise him by saying, "I have heard that you are an outstanding automobile mechanic who guarantees his work." To his affirmative response, we might well declare, "I really need you." Because we praise him for being what he is, we release him to repair our automobile.

Similarly, we search through the Yellow Pages for a roofer when our roof is leaking, and we phone the listed number. "I see in the Yellow Pages that you are a roofer and that you repair leaking roofs," we say over the phone. Because we believe him to be what and who he says he is, we release him to come and repair our roof.

When we see in the Bible that Christ is listed as the *Savior*, if we will contact Him with praise and worship for Who He declares Himself to be, we release Him to meet our need. When Peter declared Jesus to be *"the Christ, the Son of the living God,"* he was merely praising and worshiping Jesus for being Who the angels, the prophet, and the Father had declared Him to be. His worship released Jesus to minister to him as the Son of God, not as the Son of man. This could not help but initiate a higher level of worship in Peter.

This fundamental law is seen at work during the ministry of Jesus. We read, *"A man with leprosy came and knelt before* him and said, *'Lord, if you are willing, you can make me clean.'"* (Matthew 8:2). The leper worshiped Jesus as the Healer, and he released Christ to cleanse away the leprosy.

A Gentile woman *"came and worshiped Him, saying, 'Lord, help me!'"* (Matthew 15:25, NKJV). Even though she was not one of the covenant people, perhaps she had seen the advertisement in the "White Pages" of the Bible: *"God is our refuge and strength, an ever present help in trouble"* (Psalm 46:1). Her praise of Christ as a source of help brought her immediate help in her home.

Still another person outside the immediate family of Israel was a ruler, very likely a Roman, who *"came and worshiped Him, saying, 'My daughter has just died, but come and lay Your hand on her and she will live'"* (Matthew 9:18, NKJV). Had someone reported to him what had happened at the funeral at Nain or had he heard that Jesus said, *"I am the resurrection and the life. He who believes in me will live, even though he dies"* (John 11:25)? When he worshiped Jesus in His revealed nature as the source of life, he released Jesus to restore the dead daughter back to life.

It is true that there is a release of worship when we are in the Lord's presence, and it is also true that worship releases the worshiper in many wonderful ways; but it is equally true that as we worship Jesus for Who He is, our worship releases Him to become involved with us in the areas of our lives to which His worshiped nature can minister. There is nothing beyond Christ's ability, but the scope of our worship determines His availability. Worship releases God to be manifestly what He is inherently.

Revelation of Jesus releases us to worship, and worship releases further revelation to us. Worship releases us to God, and it gloriously releases God to us by allowing God to be in us Who He actually is. Perhaps the angels are called *"the holy angels"* (Matthew 25:31, NKJV) because they so consistently worship God with the praise *"Holy, holy, holy, Lord God almighty."* By their worship they release God's holiness to themselves, and they become holy.

Many persons who touched the life of Jesus learned this as they dared to worship Jesus while He was among them, for Jesus not only initiated their worship, He received it.

11

Jesus Was Worshiped

Worship did not start on earth. Long before the foundations of the world were laid, eons before Adam and Eve were placed in the garden, the angels in heaven worshiped the triune God. Whatever your concept of eternity may be, from its beginning (although eternity is without beginning or end), Jesus was an acceptable object of worship. The last book of the Bible shows Jesus being worshiped by every level of life in heaven. He has never been without worship, nor will He ever not be worshiped.

Throughout endless eternity, Jesus has received worship from heaven's celestial beings. Because eternity is not divisible by our constraints of time dimensions, it is difficult to know where the book of Revelation fits. Whether past, present, or future, it is filled with pictures of the Son of God being the object of worship. And why not? He is God!

Jesus and worship are inseparable. The Old Testament foretells it, the Gospels demonstrate it, the Epistles explain it, and the book of Revelation shows it continuing through eternity. He was worshiped as God—the God-man—God incarnate. He is the **recipient** of worship, the **reason** for worship, the **reality** of worship, and the **rebirth** of our worship. Jesus brought God from heaven to the earth and made the unseen God a visual reality by bringing us God in human flesh. It should be no great wonder, then, that the first response of those who met Immanuel was worship.

Jesus, the Recipient of Worship

In the book of Hebrews, the Holy Spirit tells us, "*And again, when God brings his firstborn into the world, he says, 'Let all God's angels worship him'*" (Hebrews 1:6). When He was an active part of the triune God, Jesus was an object of worship. After He became a man, God the Father declared His Son to still be the object of worship even in this limited form.

Not too surprisingly, then, the angels in heaven declared the divinity of Jesus here on earth. Before His conception, Gabriel told Mary, "*You will be with child and give birth to a son, and you are to give him the name Jesus. He will be great and will be called the Son of the Most High. The Lord God will give him the throne of his father David*" (Luke 1:31-32). At the birth of Jesus, the angel of the Lord declared, "*Today in the town of David a Savior has been born to you; he is Christ the Lord*" (Luke 2:11).

The Christmas story is filled with worship. Mary worshiped God with a psalm when she learned that she was pregnant by action of the Holy Spirit. Jesus has been the object of psalms, songs, shouts, and tears of worship ever since His birth. The angels worshiped from the skies above. Shepherds worshiped from the fields while tending their sheep. The wise men from the East seemed to have a revelation that this was a Great One, and they worshiped Jesus. By unction of the Holy Spirit, both Simeon and Anna recognized the Messiah in the Baby when He was brought to the Temple for dedication. They, too, worshiped although the direction of their worship was to God the Father. Still, any pollster will admit that these were a pitifully small percentage of the residents of Palestine.

Jesus, the Reason for Worship

The realistic reason Jesus is to be worshiped is that He is very God of very God, as the theologians like to put it. He cannot be separated from the Godhead except theoretically. He is as much God as the Father is God or the Spirit is God. The Son was in the beginning with the Father. In the prologue to his Gospel, the Apostle John wrote: "*In the beginning was the Word. and the Word was with God, and the Word was God*" (John 1 :1). He was the active agent in the creation of everything as we know it. We read: "*Through him all things were made; without him nothing was made that has been made*" (John 1:3). Jesus testified that the Father held nothing back from Him when He said: "*All things have been committed to me by my Father. No one knows who the Son is except the Father, and no one knows who the Father is except the Son and those to whom the Son chooses to reveal him*" (Luke 10:22).

The most vocal testimony to the divinity of Jesus came from demons on earth who came in contact with Jesus. The Gospel writers tell us, "*Moreover, demons came out of many people, shouting, 'You are the Son of God!' But he rebuked them and would not allow them to speak, because they knew he was the Christ*" (Luke 4:41). They recognized what thousands of persons missed—this man was God's Christ!

Perhaps their boss, Satan, had taught them who the Son of God was, or maybe they had experienced something in eternity about which we know nothing.

While spirit beings completely understood that this Jesus was a manifestation of the Almighty God, there seemed to be few human beings in Palestine who knew the true identity of Jesus. Even the learned religious rulers failed to comprehend that this was "Immanuel"—God with us—as announced by the angels. Christ's disciple, Peter, caught a brief glimpse of the divinity in Jesus through revelation, for he told Jesus, *"You are the Christ, the Son of the living God"* (Matthew 16:16). However, the majority saw Jesus as an anointed prophet, a miracle worker, a healer, a revolutionary, or a charlatan.

The religious leaders saw Jesus as a non-conformist and tried to ignore Him until He finally got under their skin. The teachings of Jesus often cut across the grain of the prevailing religious thought. Worse than this, Jesus demonstrated by life and action what the religious leaders only taught. This became so obvious that Jesus told the multitude, *"The teachers of the law and the Pharisees sit in Moses' seat. So you must obey them and do everything they tell you. But do not do what they do, for they do not practice what they preach"* (Matthew 23 :2-3). Little wonder, then, that the religious rulers initiated the plot to crucify Jesus.

Very soon after His birth, Jesus was thought to be a threat to King Herod's earthly position, so the king attempted to kill Him. This was a rather standard political move by a monarch threatened by a rival. Perhaps this is why Jesus must become Lord of our lives before we can successfully worship Him. Otherwise we view Him as a contender to the throne of our will.

The common people saw Jesus as an early form of welfare and Medicaid, for He met their physical needs with food and healing. The seekers after truth proclaimed Jesus a righteous man and a great teacher, but few, if any, saw Jesus as God, so they had no cause to worship Him.

Although few persons saw true divinity in the lowly carpenter's son, there were some who responded to Him in worship. They saw beyond the natural. Their spirits caught a fleeting glimpse of something far higher than themselves, and worship is always a response of the lesser to the greater.

Regardless of the people's ignorance of His identity, Jesus received worship for His performance. When men and women were delivered from demon activity, healed of leprosy, cured of blindness, or forgiven deep sins, they worshiped Him. He had proven to them His worthiness to be worshiped by what He did, not by revelation of Who He was.

Much of this worship was little more than great wonder expressed thankfully. Frequently where the *King James Version* tells us a person *"worshiped Him,"* the *New International Version* says *"He [she] kneeled down."* Yet, anemic though it was, it was worship. It recognized that one far greater than themselves was in their presence.

The beloved Apostle John told us that, *"The Word became flesh and made his dwelling among us. We have seen his glory, the glory of the One and Only, who came from the Father, full of grace and truth"* (John 1:14). Jesus so radiated divine grace that He accepted all worship no matter how elementary it might have been. He still does!

The glory that Jesus manifested by compassion, love, supernatural power, unbelievable knowledge of the Old Testament, and the ways of God became evident even to His enemies. This glory excited and incited worship responses from men, women, Jews, Gentiles, and even children. There was something so different about this man as to produce wonder in those who were around Him. This wonder often stretched into limited worship.

We have the story of the lepers who worshiped Jesus after being cleansed. The Samaritan woman at Jacob's well became a worshiper after being in the presence of Jesus for a very limited time. Mary, who poured liquid spikenard on Jesus and wiped the excess off with her hair, worshiped in an outward, emotional way. The women at the empty tomb worshiped Jesus when He revealed Himself to them, as did the disciples after He walked through barred doors to present Himself to them. Paul tells us that over 500 brethren watched the ascension of Christ in a worshipful attitude. It can comfortably be assumed that many more persons worshiped Jesus during His days on earth than the four Gospel writers record. How could persons not worship Jesus when they saw such divine glory resting on Him and flowing through Him?

Jesus, the Reality of Worship

The person of Jesus replaced the rituals of Temple worship, for it became apparent that God no longer wanted ritualistic sacrifices. From the time of Moses until the birth of Jesus, all sacrifices merely pointed to Jesus. Jesus became God's sacrificial Lamb. That's the way John the Baptist introduced his cousin: *"John saw Jesus coming toward him and said, 'Look, the Lamb of God, who takes away the sin of the world'"* (John 1:29). Who needs a substitute when the real thing is present?

Furthermore, Jesus showed us that God desired personal communion with us. Jesus, as God's Tent of Meeting, became the place where we meet God and the very God we would meet. In a most marvelous way, Jesus became both our sin bearer and our passageway into the presence of a Holy God.

The Incarnation produced far more than redemption from sin it restored our relationship with God, thereby making worship possible. Seeing God in human flesh incites us to worship, for God sent His Son Jesus, Who is God incarnate, as the reality of worship. In Him and by His authority, we dare to worship the triune God. Actually, no man can worship God in the Lord Jesus Christ until he fully believes that Jesus is truly God. If the Lord Jesus were any less than God, worshiping Him would be idolatry.

This was the point at which the Jews stumbled. They did not condemn Jesus for any wrongdoings. They told Him, "*We are not stoning you for any of these,*" replied the Jews, "*but for blasphemy, because you, a mere man, claim to be God*" (John 10:33). They had such a preconceived concept of Jehovah that when Jesus came and did not fit their profile, they totally denounced Him as an imposter.

This was also the point that caused Saul of Tarsus to be so angry against the Christians: they worshiped Jesus as God. Saul was a defender of the fundamentalist faith of his day. Jesus did not fit that view, so Saul's personal goal was to destroy all confessed believers in Jesus. He was a confessed zealot. Once he saw the Lord on the Damascus road, however, he too worshiped God through Jesus and became the great exponent of the deity and Lordship of Jesus Christ.

When God became flesh and lived here on earth as a man, He still commanded worship. Perhaps "commanded" is the wrong word, for it may produce a mental image of impulsion or compulsion. Nothing could be further from the truth. Jesus had no publicity agent. There was no TV hype heralding His coming to a city or village. Angels did not announce that God was now in the midst of His people except at the birth of Jesus when a few lowly shepherds heard them.

We cannot find a solitary incident in the Gospels where Jesus told a person to worship Him. It was not the message of Christ's forerunner, John the Baptist, and neither was it the message of the disciples. They mimicked the message of Jesus: *"Repent, for the kingdom of heaven is near"* (Matthew 4:17).

Still, without fanfare, applause signs, media hype, or heavenly messengers, Jesus was worshiped from one end of Palestine to the other. He didn't look heavenly, He didn't talk "spiritual" talk, and He certainly didn't live the life of a king or even a king's son. He was actually quite an ordinary Jew to the natural eye, but the Spirit of the Living God dwelt in that earthen body. It was like a shining light in a dark place. It was healing in the midst of sickness and comfort in the times of sorrow. The compassion of God in Christ was always in stark contrast to the harshness of the occupying Roman army. Jesus was worshiped because He was different, and the difference showed.

Jesus Is a Rebirth of Our Worship

Worship had become so codified, ritualized, and stalemated by the time Jesus came that there was little, if any, reality in it. Animals were slain, blood was sprinkled, and words were spoken, but it was empty and without emotion. Jesus brought a rebirth of worship to mankind. Far more than obeying commandments, worship became a response to a person.

It is so self-evident that Jesus still brings a new beginning to a believer's worship that little needs to be written about it. All the truly redeemed have found a loving relationship with their redeemer—the Lord Jesus Christ. It was His love that drew them to Him in the first place. They did not seek Him— He sought them and made Himself known to them. It was His grace that brought them out of their sin and the world system and taught them the joy of being forgiven. They have found a totally new life because of Jesus. As the Apostle Paul put it, *"Therefore, if anyone is in Christ, he is a new creation; the old has gone, the new has come!"* (2 Corinthians 5:17). They have not merely added God to their life—He has become their life.

Worship in its most fundamental definition is "love responding to love." Love received is returned and that is the basis of worship. Worshiping Jesus is far less the fulfillment of a command than it is the satisfying of an inner longing. Our gratitude to Him and our love for Him must find expression, and that expression is worship.

Worship does demand, however, that we accept the true person of Jesus. We must respond to Who He is declared to be, not what we picture Him to be or Who we desire Him to be. One of the curses of our generation is that we have made Jesus such a sweet, gentle, loving person that we have bypassed the truth that He is God incarnate. This is God in available form. He is God in a non-threatening image, but He is God. He is due our reverence, and whatever our purpose for drawing near Him may be, we should always bring Him the homage that is due Him.

The New Testament is full of worship expressions to Jesus. The Pauline epistles abound with praise to Christ Jesus. The general epistles rejoice in our Lord, and the book of Revelation almost drips with the enthusiastic praises of those who have entered into God's presence. Jesus is unquestionably worthy of our worship, and He rejoices to be the recipient of that worship.

There is nothing amazing about this. What is so astounding is that He, Who so consistently received worship, was Himself a worshiper.

12

Jesus Worshiped

As part of my research for this book, I talked with many Christian leaders, made e-mail contact with my computer friends, and injected into phone conversations the question, "Did Jesus worship?" I was pleased that some of them gave me several beautiful concepts of Jesus at worship. These have been incorporated into this book. I was, however, amazed at how often the response was, "I hadn't even thought of that."

We are so comfortable with the knowledge that Jesus was worshiped, and that we regularly worship Him, that we overlook the evidence in the Gospels that Jesus Himself was a worshiper. I don't suggest that Jesus danced at the front of an auditorium or waved flags and banners during a songfest, but as the perfect man, He worshiped God perfectly. While we get overwhelmed with form, Jesus was concerned with substance. We seek to produce and release a feeling, but Jesus worshiped out of an obedient relationship with His Father.

Jesus was accustomed to being worshiped. He knew the high level worship of angelic beings, and He knew the low end of worship so often expressed by those who sought only to receive a favor from Him. This intimate experiential knowledge of worship made Jesus the finest worshiper Who ever walked this earth. His love for and His devotion to His Father are exemplary.

Jesus and *Shachah* Worship

The Hebrew word most frequently used for worship in the Old Testament is *shachah. Strong's Bible Dictionary* defines *shachah*: "to depress, i.e. prostrate (especially to reflex in homage to royalty or God), bow (self) down, crouch, fall down (flat), humbly beseech, do (make) obeisance, do reverence, make to stoop, worship."

A good example of shachah worship occurs when Saul was pursuing David and inadvertently entered the cave where David and his men were hiding. David was urged by his men to kill Saul, but all David felt he dared to do was cut off part of Saul's robe. After Saul left the cave, David came out and called to him. When Saul turned to look, *"David stooped with his face to the earth, and bowed himself"* (1 Samuel 24:8, KJV). The *New International Version* says, *"David bowed down and prostrated himself with his face to the ground."* The Hebrew word used here is *shachah*—"to worship." It was an act of humble submission and recognition of the high office Saul held. Even though Saul, the man, had become David's enemy, David held Saul's office as king in the highest respect.

Jesus was the perfect worshiper in the Old Testament concept of worship. While men on earth placed Him on the highest plain, Jesus consistently held the Father on the highest level. Jesus never forgot that He was a man while He was here on the earth. He had taken on a form far lower than God, and He worshiped from this posture. He and *shachah* worship were consistently harmonious. He bowed to the will of God in His inner spirit. His outer actions merely reflected His inner attitudes.

If the fundamental meaning of *shachah* is "do reverence," Jesus is almost the personification of the word. Jesus exemplified reverence to the Father in heaven at all times and in all places. He obeyed Him, worshiped Him, prayed to Him, revealed Him, and taught the principles of God to the disciples. He declared that the words He spoke were the words He heard His Father say, and that He never exercised His own will; only the will of His Father. He even went so far as to say that the things He did were the things He saw His Father do. Such reverence! Such dedication! Such worship!

Jesus and *Proskuneo* Worship

Jesus came to earth under the Old Testament economy, but He was the pivotal turning point in worship. We could probably say that He singlehandedly ushered in the New Testament concept of worship that grew out of, but far exceeded, the Old Testament concept. While the Old Testament concept of worship was obedience, the New Testament concept was loving obedience.

The word most overwhelmingly used for *worship* in the New Testament is the Greek word proskuneo. It quite literally means "to kiss toward," as a dog licking his master's hand. It infers kissing the hand as an act of respect or worship. Again, the picture is one of submission, but it is far more intimate. It is an act of friendship or even of intimacy. It is the submission of love more than the submission to authority or duty.

Jesus had a most intimate relationship with His Father. He must certainly have been familiar with all the Old Testament names for God, but He consistently referred to Him as "Father." When He prayed, He addressed him as *Abba, Father*, or in modern English, *Papa or Daddy*. He did not bow from a distance. He approached His Father with such closeness that a kiss was possible.

How few Christians seem to come into such a personal and intimate relationship with God. We send Him an occasional fax (public prayer) or e-mail (private prayer), but Jesus worshiped in such closeness that He could kiss the Father. When Jesus responded to the request of the disciples to be taught to pray, He told them, *"When you pray, say: 'Father, hallowed be your name, your kingdom come'"* (Luke 11:2). He used the Greek word *pater* that is a familiar word for a parent. "Daddy" would be a faithful rendition. He wanted His disciples to have a sense of intimate relationship with the one they were worshiping. He still does, for this is the heart of New Testament worship.

Could there be a better demonstration of *proskuneo* worship than the way Mary, the sister of Lazarus, performed it for Jesus? Her worship was extravagant, enthusiastic, and very demonstrative, yet it proceeded from a heart of gratitude and love. She did not worship from a distance. She violated the code of her day that barred women from participation in celebration feasts and pushed her way to Jesus. She had no intention of worshiping from a distance. She had watched Jesus in honor, respect, and devotion, but when it was time to worship Him, she needed to touch Him.

As she approached Jesus, she held in her hand an alabaster box filled with costly spikenard, probably reserved for her own burial. She broke the box and poured its contents on the head of Jesus. Catching the excess as it ran down His beard, she transferred it to His feet, and then bathed those feet with her tears and wiped them clean and dry with her long hair.

Her action brought criticism from nearly every man in the room except Jesus. He knew the difference between lust and love. He was undisturbed by the extravagant tears, the excessive action, or the exorbitant expressions of love. He recognized a pure act of worship—*proskuneo* worship. He commended her and declared that this act would become a memorial for her throughout time.

Sometimes we worshipers are so "decent and in order" that we resemble the rows of white crosses in a military cemetery. No matter from what angle you choose to view them, you cannot argue with their orderliness, but there is no life there. Aren't the warmth and spontaneity of life, even if they get a little messy at times, to be preferred to the orderliness of death?

Wouldn't it be wonderful if tape recorders had been available in the days of Jesus and someone had recorded one of His all night worship sessions? We might be shocked at the outpouring of emotion, the expressions of love, and the weeping of sheer joy that formed such a part of His worship. The Messianic psalms, those psalms that point to Jesus, speak of Jesus singing, rejoicing, praising, and loving God.

On the day of Pentecost, Peter quoted from Psalm 16 and applied it to Jesus. It was recognized as a psalm pointing to the Messiah. In it we hear the Lord say, "*I will praise the LORD* ...." (Verse 7), "*Therefore my heart is glad, and my tongue rejoices*" (Verse 9). "*You have made known to me the path of life; you will fill me with joy in your presence, with eternal pleasures at your right hand*" (Verse 11). This sounds like proskuneo worship to me. It is personal and intimate, and it flows from a heart of love. Jesus was a master at this when He was in the presence of His Father. May God help us to loosen up a bit and pour out our worship similarly.

Where Jesus Worshiped

Those to whom liturgical worship is so important need to remember that Jesus was a Jew. He was reared in a pious Jewish home where all the ceremonies and rituals of Judaism were both taught and practiced. He was taken to the Temple for His circumcision, where He was worshiped by Simeon and Anna. Later, at age twelve, He went to the Temple on a feast day where he was allowed to interact with the teaching priests. The depth of His probing questions amazed these learned men.

Jesus faithfully observed the three compulsory feast days in Jerusalem with the other males of His community, for by His own words He said, "*Do not think that I have come to abolish the Law or the Prophets; I have not come to abolish them but to fulfill them*" (Matthew 5:17). Jesus was not a rebel against the Law; He was a revealer of the grace of God.

Time and time again we find Jesus in the Temple or the synagogue on the Sabbath. These were days of religious ritual and ceremony, but it was the ultimate act of worship by the Jews in that day, and Jesus was a participant.

Even after He entered His ministry, we see Him at the Temple on a feast day. We read: "*In the last day, that great day of the feast, Jesus stood and cried, saying, If any man thirst, let him come unto me, and drink. He that believeth on me, as the scripture hath said, out of his belly shall flow rivers of living water. (But this spake he of the Spirit, which they that believe on him should receive: for the Holy Ghost was not yet given; because that Jesus was not yet glorified)*" (John 7:37-39, KJV). Jesus did not reject the worship commemoration of His day, He participated in it. He earnestly sought to bring spiritual meaning to these outward acts and to introduce a higher form of worship to those who would come to actually know God, not merely know about Him.

It is most likely that anywhere Jesus found Himself to be was an apt place for worship. He didn't need the trappings many of us insist upon having before He could worship. Gothic structures, stained glass windows, pipe organs, and robed choirs were not available to Jesus, but He worshiped gloriously. He didn't need guitars, keyboards, microphones, or monitors. He had such a relationship with Father God that the waves of the sea induced worship in Him. The music of the breeze through the trees, or the sound of playing children could turn His heart to a worship mode. Even the silence of the night hours turned His heart to meditate on the Father.

To those who prefer a more free form of worship, Jesus seems to have been a free spirit. He communed with His Father in the open air. He praised and gave thanks to the Father while ministering to multitudes. He prayed both in private and in public and talked the things of God while walking from location to location. He could easily interrupt a discourse on divine things to take children on His lap and bless them without interrupting the flow of His worship, because worship was an integral part of His life. He didn't step from life to worship; His life was His worship.

Jesus also worshiped in song, for it is recorded that He sang with His disciples. The psalmist wrote: "*I will declare Your name to my brethren; in the midst of the congregation will I praise You*" (Psalm 22:22, AMP), and the Gospel writer tells us that after serving the Last Supper, "*When they had sung a hymn, they went out to the Mount of Olives*" (Matthew 26:30). Since the traditional hymn sung at the end of the Passover meal was Psalm 118, that includes the message, "*This is the day the LORD has made; let us rejoice and be glad in it*" (Psalms 118:24).

Surely Jesus would have been the one Who chose the psalm and led the singing since He didn't have a "worship leader."

Jesus spent many long nights with His disciples; often in the open air. He helped His disciples relax after a day of ministering to the people by leading them in singing psalms of worship around a campfire. In the morning hours, Jesus recited, chanted, or sang psalms unto God as He had been instructed in His childhood. If you listen closely in your spirit, you can probably hear Him joyfully cry to God:

O God, you are my God, earnestly I seek you; my soul thirsts for you, my body longs for you, in a dry and weary land where there is no water.

I have seen you in the sanctuary and beheld your power and your glory.

Because your love is better than life, my lips will glorify you.

I will praise you as long as I live, and in your name I will lift up my hands.

My soul will be satisfied as with the richest of foods; with singing lips my mouth will praise you.

On my bed I remember you; I think of you through the watches of the night.

Because you are my help, I sing in the shadow of your wings.

My soul clings to you; your right hand upholds me.

(Psalm 63:1-8)

It must have been impossible to have been around Jesus without an awareness that this man was a worshiper. His every attitude was worshipful. Everything He did was done unto His Father. He lived worship. He expressed worship inwardly and outwardly.

Could Jesus have accepted the worship of Mary and Martha in the home of Lazarus without turning this love and devotion back to His Father in worship? Perhaps one reason Jesus so frequented this home is that it had become a place of worship. Worshipers love to be around fellow worshipers.

We need to remember that Jesus came as the transitional point of moving from momentary acts of worship in God's presence to living in a state of worship. In the Old Testament context of worship, the worshiper built an altar, came to a sanctuary or, later, to the Temple. It was to be a place where God had put His name or showed Himself in one way or another. The response of the worshiper was to acknowledge that God was in that place and to respond to whatever God was doing or asking. By the time Jesus came to earth, this had been reduced to Temple forms of worship, and the presence of the LORD had not been in the Temple since before the days of Babylonian captivity.

Jesus really ended the Old Testament order of the Temple as a place of worship, and He became the place of worship where God's presence actually dwelt. His angelically proclaimed name was Emmanuel—God with us. That He had an awareness of this new role is revealed when He declared to the Jews, "*Destroy this temple, and I will raise it again in three days*" (John 2:19). They were standing near the Temple, and the Jews immediately informed Jesus, "*It has taken forty-six years to build this temple, and you are going to raise it in three days? But the temple he had spoken of was his body*" (John 2:20-21).

Jesus lived with an awareness that His Father was with Him; was actually in Him. This made Him the "temple of God." Whether awake or asleep, He was the place where worship occurred. He did not need to find God. He lived with an awareness of the continual presence of God. On the Cross when Jesus became sin on our behalf, God took His conscious presence from His Son. This was such an abnormality that Jesus cried out the prophetic words, "*My God, my God, why have you forsaken me?*" (Psalm 22:1; Matthew 27:46).

In this awareness that God dwelt in Him, everything Jesus said, did, or even thought became an act of worship. Much like the Puritans in our early American history, who lived with the concept that every act of the believer's life was to be lived as worship, Jesus lived His worship day and night. It was an act of worship when He taught, healed the sick, fed the multitude, or blessed the children. It was an act of worship as He watched the sunset over the Sea of Galilee, and even His enforced authority over the demonic realm was worship.

How sad that our busy American culture has lost sight of the indwelling of Christ in people. We localize Christ in buildings, activities, or our expressions, but we forget what Paul said: "*God has chosen to make known among the Gentiles the glorious riches of this mystery, which is Christ in you, the hope of glory*" (Colossians 1:27, emphasis added). What a mystery! What a revelation! Our hope is not in ritual, national relationship, or in behavior patterns. Our hope is the indwelling of Christ Jesus in the individual's life. He "lives in our skin" twenty-four hours of the day.

In Paul's magnanimous prayer recorded in Ephesians, he says, "*I pray that out of his glorious riches he may strengthen you with power through his Spirit in your inner being so that Christ may dwell in your hearts through faith*" (Ephesians 3:16-17). If through faith we reach an awareness that Christ really does dwell within us through the Holy Spirit, then why do we pray, praise, and worship as though He were 50,000 feet above us or fifty generations behind us? Have we not read, "*But the righteousness that is by faith says: 'Do not say in your heart, "Who will ascend into heaven?" (that is, to bring Christ down) or "Who will descend into the deep?" (that is, to bring Christ up from the dead). But what does it say? "The word is near you; it is in your mouth and in your heart," that is, the word of faith we are proclaiming"'* (Romans 10:6-8).

Worship is a response to Christ in you. God's Word asks us, *"Don't you know that you yourselves are God's temple and that God's Spirit lives in you?"* (1 Corinthians 3:16). Solomon built the great Temple in the Old Testament. Herod built the Temple that Jesus attended in the beginning of the New Testament, but God chose to build individual believers into a temple that He would inhabit through His Spirit.

Speaking of Jesus, Peter wrote: *"As you come to him, the living Stone rejected by men but chosen by God and precious to him you also, like living stones, are being built into a spiritual house to be a holy priesthood, offering spiritual sacrifices acceptable to God through Jesus Christ"* (1 Peter 2:4-5). Not only are we as individuals declared to be the temple of God, the collective body of believers is called *a spiritual house* where acceptable worship is offered to God through Jesus.

Long before Peter wrote his Epistle, Jesus knew it. He lived with a complete consciousness of the indwelling presence of the Father. He did not need to get outside Himself to commune with God. He and God had an intimate inner companionship.

The analogy to Jesus is obvious. He is *the living stone* and we have been built together as living stones. Doesn't this assure us that the true place for worship is the life of the believer? It is, of course, proper for us to go to church, but we should not need to go there in order to worship. We go there to celebrate worship with other believers. If there has been no song in our hearts during the six days of the week, it is highly improbable that there will be a song unto the Lord on Sunday morning. If our spirit has not breathed prayer and praise when we were in private, we are not qualified to do so in public. We do not come to church to meet Jesus. He lives within us. We bring Him to church with us.

From His entrance into our time/space capsule, Jesus became the pattern that leads us to experience true worship. We respond to God not in a temple made with hands, but in a temple made of living stones—the inner sanctuary of our own lives. The life of Jesus was not merely filled with acts of worship, He continually walked in a state of worship. He had intimate communion and fellowship with the God within Himself.

We need to cultivate this awareness of "Christ in you" until our conscious mind naturally turns to Jesus whenever it is not occupied with something else. When we think on Him, we respond to Him. Prayer, praise, and worship should be as natural an instinct in us as it was in Jesus. Worship should be the imminent or inherent response of our soul to the life-giver. It was in the life of Jesus!

Jesus may have worshiped to fulfil the command of the Old Testament, but I believe His worship flowed out of a deep seated need in His life. The same reasons that caused Jesus to worship should drive us into the presence of God for regular adoration of His divine person. You see, although Jesus was God, He came as a servant, and servants need to comfortably come to grips with their relationship to and with their masters—don't we?

13

Jesus, The Servant of God, Worshiped

We are told to "*serve the Lord*" nineteen times in as many verses in the Bible. David put it so succinctly when he taught Israel to sing, "*Serve the LORD with fear and rejoice with trembling*" (Psalms 2:11). The Hebrew word we have translated into fear is *yirah* which means "reverence." It is a much used worship word in the Bible. David, under the inspiration of the Holy Spirit, was pleading with Israel, and us, to worship with a three-fold thrust: (1) service, (2) reverence, and (3) rejoicing.

The service and rejoicing must flow out of reverence. All our service must be unto God or it is not worship. Similarly, our rejoicing is in the Lord; not merely in our benefits from the Lord. Service is the response of a servant or slave. Rejoicing is the response of a celebrant, but God has not set it up as an either/or option. We serve the Lord with gladness and we serve Him in our rejoicing. This is gloriously demonstrated in the earthly life of Jesus.

Jesus, God's Servant

In discussing Christ's humbling of Himself to become a man, Paul said, *"Who,* [Jesus] *being in very nature God, did not consider equality with God something to be grasped, but made himself nothing, taking the very nature of a servant, being made in human likeness"* (Philippians 2:6-7, emphasis added). Many other translators use the term slave or bond slave.

In that day of Roman rule when slavery was the normal work force, Paul's word *slave* would be fully understood. It was the bottom of the social scale; indeed, it was "nothing." Jesus gave up all volitional rights and became an unpaid slave to Father God. It was not enough that Jesus traded being God for being a man; He traded the freedom of being a man for the role of a slave.

Jesus magnificently characterizes the Old Testament slave who, upon becoming eligible for his freedom, volunteered to stay on as a servant for life. His master pierced his ear and inserted an earring so that all who came in contact with him would know that he was now a love slave (see Deuteronomy 15:16-17).

The word *servant* to the American mind is demeaning. We can accept being called an employee, but we are offended if someone calls us a servant. We've even upgraded the titles for workers who perform menial tasks. Janitors are now called custodians. Garbage collectors have taken on the title of sanitation engineers, and most men have now learned the penalty for calling a married woman a housewife, for she is now properly called a homemaker. None of this is wrong. It is proper to give dignity to a worker. What is important is that the worker do his or her job efficiently and timely. It is the task, not the title, that is important.

There are many titles given to Jesus by different religions and by the Church, and they all have foundation in the Scriptures. He is called Savior, Redeemer, Healer, Friend, Shepherd, and many other endearing terms. A plaque hanging in my office lists 35 other names and titles for our Lord Jesus. Yet for all these descriptive titles for Jesus, one rarely sees the title *servant of God*, even though the New Testament calls Jesus a servant in testimony, sermon, and prayer.

In his sermon on the day of Pentecost, Peter told the assembled Jews: *"The God of Abraham, Isaac and Jacob, the God of our fathers, has glorified his servant Jesus,"* and later he declared, *"When God raised up his servant, he sent him first to you to bless you by turning each of you from your wicked ways"* (Acts 3:13, 26, emphasis added).

Peter and John returned to the believers after they had been released from prison. In a prayer of rejoicing, they prayed to God: *"Indeed Herod and Pontius Pilate met together with the Gentiles and the people of Israel in this city to conspire against your holy servant Jesus, whom you anointed"* (Acts 4:27, emphasis added). The *King James* translators had chosen to say *"holy child Jesus,"* but most modern translators, having access to better Greek manuscripts, prefer the term holy servant.

Just three verses later, the disciples prayed: *"Stretch out your hand to heal and perform miraculous signs and wonders through the name of your holy servant Jesus"* (Acts 4:30, emphasis added). Here, again, current translators use servant where the older translators used child.

Please recognize that this title is given by men who loved, lived with, and assisted Jesus in His ministry. More than anyone else, Peter and John were in a position to see Jesus function, and they felt He behaved as a servant.

Even Paul, whose knowledge of Jesus came through divine revelation, called Jesus a servant. He told the Church at

Rome, "*For I tell you that Christ has become <u>a servant of the</u> <u>Jews on behalf of God's truth</u>, to confirm the promises made to the patriarchs*" (Romans 15:8, emphasis added). Paul understood what he was saying, for he began his New Testament epistles with such phrases as, "*Paul the servant of Jesus Christ,*" "*Paul, the prisoner of Jesus,*" or "*Paul an Apostle of Jesus*" (the word apostle simply means "sent one").

James, Peter, Jude, and John also called themselves servants of the Lord. Does this title seem demeaning to you? God used it to describe Job, Moses, David, and most of the prophets. More amazing, though, is that in the book of Isaiah, God, looking ahead, called Jesus His servant when He said: "*Here is my servant, whom I uphold, my chosen one in whom I delight; I will put my Spirit on him and he will bring justice to the nations*" (Isaiah 42:1).

Worship Flows Out of Servanthood

Remember, the Hebrew word most frequently used for worship in the Old Testament is *shachah*. It basically means "to bow down in honor and homage." It is not too involved with exuberance and excitement; it is concerned with an expressed attitude of submissive relationship. It is the lesser bowing to the greater. A friend of mine who has faithfully studied the Hebrew language tells me that the word carries with it the feeling of a servant. It connotes a submissive experience.

If worship is submission to God, Jesus fits the definition perfectly. Was anyone more of a servant of God than Jesus? Five times in the first four chapters of the book of Acts, Jesus is called a servant, even "your holy servant." In every way, Jesus was completely subservient to the will of God. We read, "'*My food,' said Jesus,' is to do the will of him who sent me and to finish his work*'" (John 4:34). John also reported Jesus as saying: "*For I have come down from heaven not to do my will but to do the will of him who sent me*" (John 6:38).

This absolute surrender of His volition to the will of His Father is the highlight of His prayer in the Garden of Gethsemane. In the hours preceding His crucifixion, Jesus prayed: *"Abba, Father . . . everything is possible for you. Take this cup from me. Yet not what I will, but what you will"* (Mark 14:36). This prayer of submission followed a life lived in submission to God. It was merely the verbalization of a truth. The ministry of Jesus was the heart of His worship, because everything He did was an expression of His submission to the will of His Father. The deeds merely expressed the inner heart of faith and obedience to the known will of God. Jesus knew better than we that true worship is a lifestyle far more than it is a musical expression of joy. There couldn't be a more complete fulfillment of Paul's entreaty, *"Therefore, I urge you, brothers, in view of God's mercy, to offer your bodies as living sacrifices, holy and pleasing to God—this is your spiritual act of worship. Do not conform any longer to the pattern of this world, but be transformed by the renewing of your mind. Then you will be able to test and approve what God's will is his good, pleasing and perfect will"* (Romans 12:1-2, emphasis added).

Submitting our lives to the perfect will of God is a genuine spiritual act of worship. No amount of singing, praising, or dancing will qualify as worship without it. Jesus became for us a perfect example of being a living sacrifice; holy and pleasing to God (spiritual act of worship).

We, Too, Are Servants Of God

While Jesus was our example of servanthood, He did not become our substitute in this. We, too, are servants of God. God calls us *"his servants"* and *"my servants"* (Revelation 1:1; 2:20), and Peter directs us to *"live as servants of God"* (1 Peter 2:16). The promise of the outpouring of the Spirit is, *"Even on my servants, both men and women, I will pour out my Spirit in those days, and they will prophesy*" (Acts 2:1,8 emphasis added). In Paul's day even the demons knew that he and his fellow workers were "*servants of the Most High God*" (Acts 16:17). The concept is not even open for discussion. We are the servants of God. He says so and that settles it!

But how does being a servant and being a worshiper correlate? Isn't this the same contrast we find in Mary and Martha? Mary was a worshiper, while Martha was a worker; a servant. Mary sat at the feet of Jesus, while Martha prepared a meal for Him. When Martha complained to Jesus about Mary's lack of participation in the kitchen, Jesus told her, "*You are worried and upset about many things, but only one thing is needed. Mary has chosen what is better, and it will not be taken away from her*" (Luke 10:41-42). Many persons have interpreted this as placing service in a depreciative position. Isn't Jesus merely telling her what He had told the devil during the time of temptation: "*Worship the Lord your God and serve him only*" (Luke 4:8). It is a matter of priority: worship first; service second. When Jesus is present, we worship. When we go from His presence we do what He instructed us to do.

The psalmists knew this balance, for they wrote: "*Praise the LORD, all you servants of the LORD,*" and "*Praise him, you servants of the Lord*" (Psalm 134:1; 135:1). It is never a choice between the two. We serve out of worship and we worship in our service. How beautifully Jesus demonstrated this.

There are three fundamental functions expected of a servant: listening to instructions, implementing those instructions, and reporting the results.

Servants Listen to Instructions

David wrote, "*As the eyes of slaves look to the hand of their master, as the eyes of a maid look to the hand of her mistress, so our eyes look to the LORD our God, till he shows* us his mercy," and "*My eyes are ever on the LORD*" (Psalms 123:2; 25:15). He understood the importance of a servant's anticipation of being needed. He had servants constantly looking for his signal, and he wanted to have a Godward gaze just in case there was something God wanted him to do. Jesus certainly kept this gaze. He was ever alert to the will of His Father.

Servants are not independent contractors. They do what they are told to do, and they stay within the parameters that are set for them. Jesus testified, "*For I did not speak of my own accord, but the Father who sent me commanded me what to say and how to say it. I know that his command leads to eternal life. So whatever I say is just what the Father has told me to say*" (John 12:49-50).

What discipline! What control! Jesus recognized Himself to be the messenger of a divine communique, not the originator of one. He said what the Father told Him to say and then remained silent. He told the people, "*These words you hear are not my own, they belong to the Father who sent me*" (John 14:24)

How difficult this is. When we hear God speak a word to us, we very often enlarge it, embellish it, personalize it, and make a full sermon out of it. That is not servanthood. It is closer to plagiarism or, even worse, it is putting words in God's mouth. It is saying, "God said," when He did not say it.

How could Jesus restrict His teaching to the things He heard His Father say? By spending time in the presence of God and waiting silently to hear His voice, Jesus learned the secret of two-way communication in prayer. He didn't do all the talking, for He, better than we, knew how very little we learn when talking. Learning comes from listening. Of course there is a place for the shout in worship, but it is very difficult to hear God when we are shouting at the top of our lungs.

Jesus was so conscious of the indwelling presence of God through the Holy Spirit that He could hear God whisper gently in all kinds of situations. The consistent attitude of worship in which Jesus lived kept Him conscious of God's voice. Jesus didn't have to memorize what the Father had said the night before. He could hear the voice of the Father while in the midst of service as a servant.

The present body of Christ needs to learn the discipline of not saying "God said" until we have heard God say it. What pain we would be spared if we would stop trying to function as "God's representatives" and return to being "God's servants." We would then speak and do only as we had been instructed.

Servants Implement Instructions

Jesus, the Servant of God, not only restricted His words to what He heard the Father speak, He confined His actions to God's will. He said, "*I tell you the truth, the Son can do nothing by himself; he can do only what he sees his Father doing, because whatever the Father does the Son also does. For the Father loves the Son and shows him all he does*" (John 5:19-20).

This, of course, required that Jesus spend sufficient time in God's presence to know what the Father was doing. In His times of worship, faith enabled Him to see beyond the present into the perfect will of God.

Jesus said, "*Don't you believe that I am in the Father, and that the Father is in me? The words I say to you are not just my own. Rather, it is the Father, living in me, who is doing his work*" (John 14:10). Not only was it the indwelling God Who gave Jesus the words to speak, but God also did great works through Jesus. These were often called "the works of God."

I believe it was Dwight L. Moody who said, "The secret to success in ministry is to find out what God is doing, and do it with Him" How much energy we waste telling God what we purpose to do, and then ask Him to "bless it." Why should God bless our activities? We are the servants, not the masters. It is our responsibility to find out what He is about to do and find our place in doing it with Him. Jesus never missed because He knew in advance what was going to be done. His awareness of the continual abiding presence of His Father made Him the channel for service of great and mighty works all glorifying God.

Worship is a time of hearing and seeing into the spiritual world. It is our first responsibility as servants of God. We cannot speak for Him or do His works without this spiritual sensitivity. Servants must first listen, then they obey.

God does not speak merely to increase our levels of knowledge and understanding. We are not college students; we are servants. Although Jesus was a great teacher, that was not the main purpose of His incarnation. He came to do the will of God. He did not write prayer journals; He implemented His Father's instruction. He was less interested in prophetic utterance than He was absorbed in doing the will of God. What is God saying today? What are we doing about it?

Servants Report the Results

When a master gave instructions to a servant, he expected immediate and implicit response. He assumed the servant would report the results of that action. Jesus was faithful in this. We find Jesus spending a night in prayer after most of His major ministries. For whatever other reasons He might have had, it seems logical that He would be giving His Father a report on the day's mighty activities.

Luke records: *"At that time Jesus, full of joy through the Holy Spirit, said, 'I praise you, Father, Lord of heaven and earth, because you have hidden these things from the wise and learned, and revealed them to little children. Yes, Father,*

135

for this was your good pleasure' " (Luke 10:21). It was with rejoicing that Jesus reported the response to His teaching.

It is not by accident that the order of entering into God's presence is given as: *"Enter his gates with thanksgiving and his courts with praise; give thanks to him and praise his name"* (Psalm 100:4). Servants first report their obedient actions with thanksgiving, then they are sufficiently discharged from pride to really praise their Lord.

It is difficult to solemnly worship out of inactivity. Jesus asked: *"Why do you call me, 'Lord, Lord,' and do not do what I say?"* (Luke 6:46). Too often we are like the servant who did nothing with the money (talent) given to him by his master. How often we have received gifts from God's Spirit, graces from God's Son, and direction from God's Word, but we have done nothing with them. Isn't it hypocrisy to enter into forms of worship when we have nothing but rebellion and inactivity to report to the Master?

In the Garden, just before His arrest and crucifixion, Jesus reported to His Father, *"I have brought you glory on earth by completing the work you gave me to do"* (John 17:4). That is the proper report of a true servant. We sing and shout, "I give You glory," but Jesus knew that obedience as a servant is what gives glory to God, not the shallow singing of carnal Christians.

The great commendation we all yearn to hear is, *"Well done, good and faithful servant! You have been faithful with a few things; I will put you in charge of many things. Come and share your master's happiness!"* (Matthew 25:21). It is "well done," not well sung.

Jesus was the perfect servant worshiper. He worshiped out of need to know His Father's will, and out of a sincere desire to faithfully perform that will. Jesus was also the Son of man, and this created the base for a different motivation for worship.

14

Jesus, the Son of Man, Worshiped

The phrase "son of man" is a familiar Old Testament expression. The psalmists used it in their poetry, and the Spirit used it in addressing God's servants. In the book of Ezekiel, this great prophet is called "son of man" eighty-eight times. Is it a mere coincidence that Jesus is called "Son of man" in the New Testament eighty-eight times? Eighty-four of those times are in the Gospels. Possibly the Holy Spirit sought to underscore the humanity of Jesus without diminishing His calling, anointing, or special relationship to God.

It seems impossible for a person to read the Gospels without perceiving that from before His sinless birth through His substitutionary sacrifice on the cross and subsequent resurrection and ascension, Jesus was the object of worship from creatures in heaven and persons on earth. What was His attitude? How did He handle it? Many of our sports heros and entertainment stars have discovered that crowd adulation is pretty heady wine. It can seriously alter one's personality and self-image. It does not appear that this happened to Jesus. The men who spent years traveling with Him daily do not report any signs of altered personality because of the praise and worship of persons to whom He ministered. He never lost contact with His humanity. He remained comfortable in the presence of saints and sinners—rich and poor—men and women—children and the aged. The praise of others never produced pride in Him.

This cuts across the grain of the human personality. When hundreds of persons declare your greatness, it is difficult to not believe them, unless a deliberate choice is made to discount this praise. Jesus made this choice. He never lost sight of Who He was. He didn't embrace a false humility, nor did He depreciate the worshipers as being uniformed or overenthusiastic. He learned the ability to receive praise and, in turn, give it back to God. He could defuse the power of adulation without being damaged by it. He simply gave it all to His Father. We can do the same thing, if we will discipline ourselves to do so.

Jesus Became a Man to Reveal the Father

Jesus was, indeed, a worshiper, but why? He was the Son of God and equal with the Father. He had been active in the creation of all things—even the human race that was now bowing before Him in worship. Since He was the deserving recipient of worship, why did He feel it necessary to be a worshiper Himself?

Paul, the great scriptural theologian, wisely said, *"Beyond all question, the mystery of godliness is great: He appeared in a body, was vindicated by the Spirit, was seen by angels, was preached among the nations, was believed on in the world, was taken up in glory*" (1 Timothy 3:16). Perhaps this was one of Paul's great understatements: "**The mystery of godliness is great.**"

Jesus did not come and take over an existing man's body. This seems to be what happened to Samson, for where we read, "*The Spirit of the LORD came mightily upon him*" (Judges 14:6; 15:14, KJV), the literal rendering of the Hebrew is "*The Spirit of the LORD clothed Himself with Samson.*" It was God invading Samson and doing through him what Samson lacked the ability to do. This was convenient, but temporary, as Samson's lifestyle proves. When God clothed Himself with Samson, this Israelite could do mighty deeds, but without God's divine invasion, he could not live a righteous life.

God did not merely take on the form of a human in the coming of Jesus as in Old Testament theophanic manifestations where God appeared as a man in order to communicate with persons without creating a great fear barrier. This occurred on repeated occasions, as when the three men appeared to Abraham.

Jesus was neither a theophany nor a normal person invaded by the Spirit of God. He actually became a person. He was conceived in Mary's womb, gestated there, and was delivered in birth in Bethlehem of Judah where Mary placed Him in a manger. It was necessary for Him to grow and mature as any other mortal. Dr. Luke assures us: "*And the child grew and became strong; he was filled with wisdom, and the grace of God was upon him*" (Luke 2:40). Like any baby, Jesus had to mature into manhood as multitudes before and after Him have done. But why?

Jesus could not be compared to any other person, for "*He (God) was made visible in human flesh*" (1 Timothy 3:16, AMP). Something had to be done to enable men to relate to

God. When God spoke directly to the people at Mt. Sinai, they responded in such fear that they, through their representatives, asked God to never speak directly to them again, lest they die (see Deuteronomy 5:24-27). God accommodated their request. Instead of a relationship where He talked with them, He gave them written codes to follow and rituals to observe to maintain their standing in His covenant.

When something not covered by the written code needed to be declared, God sent angels with a message, but there was still a response of fear from those who saw the angels. They usually recoiled in fright expecting to die, for these messengers were so unearthly. To handle this barrier, God then spoke to the Israelites through the prophets, but when the people did not like their message, they stoned them to death. God was experiencing great difficulty communing with His children in a relational manner. It may almost have been through desperation that God determined to become like us in hopes that we would hear and lovingly respond to Him.

God may have thought, "If I become what they are, they will understand and relate to Me." So God became a man and we called His name Jesus. When Paul wrote his letter to the church at Philippi, he explained Christ's choice to lay aside His divine prerogatives to function as an anointed man. He wrote:

> *Your attitude should be the same as that of Christ Jesus:*
>
> *Who, being in very nature God, did not consider equality with God something to be grasped,*
>
> *but made himself nothing, taking the very nature of a servant, being made in human likeness.*

*And being found in appearance as a man, he
humbled himself and became obedient to death
even death on a cross!*

*Therefore God exalted him to the highest
place and gave him the name that is above every
name, that at the name of Jesus every knee should
bow, in heaven and on earth and under the earth,*

*and every tongue confess that Jesus Christ is
Lord, to the glory of God the Father.*

(Philippians 2:5-11)

Theologians calls this the *Kenosis* or self-emptying of
Christ. There was never a point when He was not God, nor
was there ever a moment when He functioned as God. He
laid aside His divinity to become a commoner.

We often overlook the truth that the ministry Jesus shared
was the ministry of an anointed person. This is strongly
underscored in the words of Jesus to His disciples, "*I tell you
the truth, anyone who has faith in me will do what I have
been doing. He will do even greater things than these, because
I am going to the Father*" (John 14:12). One need not be a
God-man to do what Jesus did. He can have the same anointing
that rested upon Jesus, for all the works of Jesus were done as
an anointed man of God. He had emptied Himself and
voluntarily laid aside His divine attributes to function one-
hundred percent as a man.

Jesus Was a Puzzle to His Disciples

While He was here on the earth, He was not seated on
the throne in heaven. He was not everywhere present while
walking from Jerusalem to Galilee. Some could see that He

141

was divine, but He chose to live, love, and labor as a person. What kind of person was He?

The incident of Jesus calming the storm at sea was so indelibly written in the minds of the disciples that three of the Gospel writers record it in considerable detail. When Jesus stood in the sinking boat and rebuked the wind and the waves, producing a great calm, the disciples asked,

"*What kind of man is this?*" (Matthew 8:27), and "*Who is this?*" (Mark 4:41; Luke 8:25). The *King James Bible* translates the Greek as "*What manner of man is this?*" The disciples were at a loss to categorize Jesus. He didn't fit any classifications of humanity that were familiar to them.

They knew Him as a man who hungered, thirsted, enjoyed life, was gentle with women and children, and was compassionate with the sick and the needy. They had seen Him angry, and they had watched Him weep over Jerusalem. They enjoyed His companionship, for He was very much a man's man and a true leader of men. They knew His mother, had met His brothers and sisters, and were aware of His skills as a carpenter, but there was something more—an indefinable something.

They had watched Him turn water into wine, heal the sick, restore sight to the blind, and even raise the dead, and now they watched His amazing authority over nature. They exclaimed in fearful bewilderment: "*Who is this? Even the wind and the waves obey him!*" (Mark 4:41).

The disciples may have been among the first to discover that they could not categorize Jesus, but they were certainly not the last. Men through the ages have been puzzled at this amazing combination of God and man. He has human names and He has divine names. He is called the Son of David and the Son of God. He always was and yet we know His birthplace was Bethlehem of Judea. He worshiped the Father and yet He Himself became the object of worship. He was not a split personality, nor was He two persons functioning as one; this was the God-man. He was always all God, and He was equally all man at all times. The world has no precedent for this man, for He is unique—the special Begotten of the Father.

Jesus Worshiped Out of Choice

Complex as this is, it gives us a strong clue as to *why* Jesus worshiped. As a man, He needed to worship. It discharged the pride-producing praise of people, and kept His human spirit rightly related to the divine God. The more adulation He received, the more He needed to pass this on to Father God.

In my earlier traveling ministry, I did not know how to handle people's praise. I would tell them, "Don't thank me. Give the praise to the Lord." It sounded so righteous, but it often cut the individual right to the heart.

One day when I was in prayer, the Lord asked me in my spirit why I was so hard on persons who expressed thanks and appreciation to me. He told me that instead of rebuking them, or making them feel that they had done something wrong, I should graciously receive all praise and, in turn, hand it to God.

I learned to make a bouquet of these praises. Now each night before going to sleep, I present this bouquet of praises to the Lord. It gives me some "glory" to present to Him, and it gets it out of my system before I have time to believe that I am worthy of praise and react in pride.

This was one reason the Son of man spent time in worship of the Father. He wanted to pass on to God what had been so lovingly presented to Him. Jesus, Whose teachings showed a great familiarity with the Psalter, would certainly have been acquainted with the injunction of Psalm 47:6-7: *"Sing praises to God, sing praises; sing praises to our King, sing praises. For God is the King of all the earth; sing to him a psalm of praise."*

Far too frequently we fail to realize that praise can flow out of our choice to praise. We don't need an emotional stimuli or great awareness of the presence of God to praise Him. We are creatures of choice. We can choose to praise the Lord. Jesus did!

In the Messianic twenty-second Psalm, we read, *"I will declare your name to my brothers; in the congregation I will praise you"* (Psalm 22:22). This verse is quoted in the book of Hebrews where it reads: *"I will declare your name to my brothers; in the presence of the congregation I will sing your praises"* (Hebrews 2:12). In both instances there is strong emphasis on the expression of the will of Jesus *"I will declare your name"* —*"I will praise you"*—*"I will sing your praises."* Jesus didn't need to be stimulated to worship. He had set His will to be a worshiper.

Jesus praised and worshiped when His ministry was received and when it was rejected. He worshiped when His disciples were cooperative and when they were cantankerous. He worshiped in the Temple with other worshipers, and He worshiped in private on the seashore. He worshiped with laughter and with silence. He worshiped in joy and in pain, for He had learned that worship is a choice. Worship is always far more concerned with our perceived relationship to God than our emotional sensations. Jesus, the man, made a conscious decision to worship God. So can we!

Jesus Worshiped Out of Obedience

In explaining that Jesus came to replace the temple rituals and sacrifices, the writer of the book of Hebrews quotes Psalm 40:7: *"Then I said, 'Here I am it is written about me in the* scroll—*I have come to do your will, O God*'" (Hebrews 10:7). That Jesus, the Servant of God, was obedient is obvious. Equally conspicuous is the fact that Jesus, the Son of man, set Himself to obey the will of Father God. Jesus knew that the injunction given to King Saul was as real now as it was then. Through the prophet, God told Saul, *"To obey is better than sacrifice, and to heed is better than the fat of rams"* (1 Samuel 15:22).

God began the Ten Commandments with, *"You shall have no other gods before me"* (Exodus 20:3), and when the law was repeated to the second generation, God said, *"Hear, O Israel: The LORD our God, the LORD is one. Love the LORD your God with all your heart and with all your soul and with all your strength"* (Deuteronomy 6:4-5). This would be worship at its highest level and it is not a suggestion. It is a commandment made by God. Jesus accepted it as such.

Every time we read *"Praise the Lord"* we are looking at a command. The frequent cries in the Bible, *"Worship the Lord,"* are divine directives that cannot be ignored with impunity. Jesus knew this, so He humbled Himself to be obedient to them. He worshiped the Father out of an obedient response.

Do you suppose that there were days that He just didn't have time to worship? Were there seasons when He felt too tired to give Himself to worship? He was human and subject to hunger and fatigue. In order to regain strength, He occasionally withdrew from the multitudes and took His disciples into uninhabited regions to rest. There is no reason to believe that this interfered with His obedient response of worship. Since His worship was to the Father who was in Him at all times, Jesus could even worship on His vacation. He desired to get away from needy people, but He never felt the compulsion to take a rest from the presence of God.

In every way, Jesus, the Son of man, was perfectly obedient to God, which means that He must have been a perfect worshiper of God. What was it that drove the Son of God to worship?

15

Jesus, The Son Of God, Worshiped

Even for persons with a limited knowledge of the Gospels, accepting Jesus as the perfect man is not difficult. He was, as He frequently said, *"The Son of man."* Even His enemies accredited Him with greatness as a humanitarian, teacher, miracle worker, and provider.

The thing about Jesus that rubbed raw the emotions of the religious rulers of His day was not His deeds, but His claim to being the Son of God. We read that after Jesus healed the lame man at the pool of Bethesda: *"For this reason the Jews tried all the harder to kill him; not only was he breaking the Sabbath, but he was even calling God his own Father, making himself equal with God"* (John 5:18, emphasis added).

Jesus was not crucified for anything He did. At His trial, Pilate found nothing wrong with His behavior and sought to release Him, but *"The Jews insisted, 'We have a law, and according to that law he must die, because he claimed to be the Son of God'"* (John 19:7).

This concept is what sparked the horrible persecution of the early Christians. The declaration that "Jesus Christ is Lord" was provocative enough to have a person thrown to the lions, burned at the stake, or imprisoned for life. To call Jesus the Son of God was considered downright heresy, and religious zealots like Saul of Tarsus sought to stamp it out by killing the adherents of that doctrine.

Jesus, Inseparable from God

Still, if we embrace the unity of the Trinity, we must believe in the full deity of the Lord Jesus. It is not merely that God the Son dwells in the Father in the way that we are associated with God, but the three persons of the Godhead are ONE. God the Son existed eternally before He came into the world as a man. There could be no eternal Father without an eternal Son and no eternal Son without the eternal Father. The very Spirit of God is called *"the eternal Spirit"* (Hebrews 9:14).

The Scriptures teach that although Jesus was perfect God and perfect man, He was one person. Our Lord Jesus Christ as the Son of God existed from eternity, and when He chose to enter this world that He had made, He did not take a human person into union with Himself; He took a human nature. The Son of God became the Son of man. Nowhere is it said that a son of man became God. Just as the seat of personality in a human being is in his spiritual nature, the seat of personality in the God-man is in His divine nature.

The disciples did not understand the communion of attributes in Christ Jesus. One nature did not participate in the attributes of the other. Therefore, the human nature did not become omnipresent, nor did the divine nature share in the weakness and limitation of knowledge characteristic to human nature. The person of Christ Jesus was the partaker of the attributes of both natures. What was true of either nature, or of the two combined as the God-man, was true of the person of Christ.

What the disciples could not comprehend through observation, Paul was able to grasp through revelation, for he wrote, *"It pleased the Father that in Him all the fullness should dwell,"* and *"In Him dwells all the fullness of the Godhead bodily"* (Colossians 1:19; 2:9, NKJV). Perhaps we, who are on the far side of Calvary, do not understand it much better than the disciples did. Even what we cannot truly conceive, we may receive through faith in what God has told us: *"Jesus Christ is Lord"* (Philippians 2:11).

Jesus, the Image of God

In his great resurrection discourse, Paul makes a strong contrast between Adam and Jesus. He says, *"So it is written: 'The first man Adam became a living being'; the last Adam, a life-giving spirit. . . . The first man was of the dust of the earth, the second man from heaven"* (1 Corinthians 15:45, 47). Paul reminds us that although the Adam in the Garden of Eden was made "in the image of God," he was actually formed out of the dust of the earth. Jesus, Who came in the image of God, had His origins in heaven.

The great theologian, Paul, also says that the man out of the dust was the first Adam, but Jesus was the last Adam. Because the first Adam and his sin-deformed progeny failed so completely in comprehending and revealing the invisible God, the divine councils of heaven decreed an end to the lineage of Adam. Jesus came as the last of the Adams, in order to eradicate once and for all the irreversible failure of man to reveal the divine Father. Although millions of people had been born between Adam and Jesus, God's image in them was so marred by sin that it was defaced, defiled, and deformed unrecognizably.

When God chose to reveal His image in the second man, He gave him a different nature—a higher nature. The first man was made in the image of God as Lincoln's image is imprinted on our penny, but the second man is the image of God as Lincoln's son bore his father's image: "*Christ, who is the image of God*" (2 Corinthians 4:4). Whereas the first Adam was a man made in the image of God, Jesus was God, "*bearing the human likeness, revealed in human shape*" (Philippians 2:8, NEB). Instead of trying to elevate man into the divine image, God reversed the process by beginning with the image of God and placing it in human flesh. Thus Adam was replaced by Jesus, Who not only ended the Adams, but also began an entirely new lineage by becoming the "second man" the God-man.

Wouldn't this give us a clue about the way the Son of God worshiped God the Father? The Adam in the Garden of Eden lived a life of worship. Everything he did, until the day of his rebellion, was an obedient response to God. In the cool of the day, Adam and Eve walked with God and talked the things of life. There is no Bible evidence that they talked great spiritual truths. They communed about the everyday things that concerned Adam. It was not so much the content of their communication as it was the fellowship they enjoyed while talking that became worship.

This is the relationship the "last Adam" had with God. They enjoyed sharing life. They walked together, talked together, enjoyed sunsets together, and laughed together.

Jesus Lived His Worship

Jesus did not need to withdraw from life in order to worship. He lived a life of worship. Everything He did was an expression of the living relationship He enjoyed with His Father. He, better than we, realized that all creation worships God when it functions in the realm for which it was created. The rose bush worships when it blossoms a rose. The clouds worship when they pour down rain. People worship when they are what God ordained that they should be in this life. It is not worship of God to go to Indonesia as a missionary if the will of God for your life is to be a carpenter in Topeka, Kansas.

When we go to church on Sunday to "worship," we've actually ceased from worship and have gathered to celebrate worship. If there has been no worship of God during the week if our lives have been lived selfishly and without thought of God, it is highly improbable that we will worship on Sunday. If there has been no song unto God for six days, why do we think we will sing with meaning on the seventh?

Rev. Shirley Carpenter, a friend of mine, shared with me a meditation she had recently. Being musically inclined and preaching much on worship, she asked the Lord to reveal to her the highest realm of musical expression in the Old Testament. She felt challenged to mentally review the worship of the Old Testament Tabernacle. She remembered the great choirs David had trained that sang in the outer court. She could almost hear the chanting of the priests as they offered sacrifices to God, but she knew the highest realm of worship was offered by the High Priest in the Holy of Holies.

As she meditated on the High Priest's entrance into this holy place on the day of Atonement, she realized that when he went through the door to the holy place, all sound was muted. There was no song in this inner court. There were no shouts or chants. The lamps flickered quietly, and the incense on the golden altar sent its fragrance without a sound.

As the priest walked through the veil into the Holy of Holies with a basin of blood from the outer court in one hand and a censer of incense from the inner court in his other hand, the only sound to be heard was the muted ring from the golden bells on the skirt of his robe as they collided with the pomegranates that were interspersed between the bells. It was the priest's walk, not his talk, that God saw as the highest worship. Why have we felt that our lips are more important than our lives? Jesus didn't. His walk was the worship heaven listened to.

Jesus Was Dependent Upon God

It is probably self-evident that Jesus was dependent upon His Father for spiritual energy, wisdom, and ministry. His worship life was the thing that energized Him, not His ministry. Healing the multitudes was done out of sheer obedience. Jesus drew life from the Father, not from earthly adulation. People drained Jesus just as they do anyone who has a true spiritual ministry. When the woman with the issue of blood touched the hem of Jesus' garment, *"at once Jesus realized that power had gone out from him. He turned around in the crowd and asked, 'Who touched my clothes?'"* (Mark 5:30). His spiritual life and energy came from His intimate relationship with His Father from worship. That energy was shared with others when He ministered to them.

What may be less obvious is that Jesus needed a continual relationship with His Father to fulfill His need to worship. There are a variety of descriptive phrases attached to Jesus. Among them is the one used twice in the book of Acts where the apostles speak of *"your holy servant Jesus"* (Acts 4:27,30). In an earlier book of mine, I wrote:

> This matter of being holy is far more than a deep religious feeling. It radically affects our lifestyle. It is concerned with our attitudes, actions, associations, adoration, thoughts, love, obedience level, and even our marriage partner. Holiness is a governing principle of life to be manifested in every area of life as displayed inwardly and outwardly towards God, our self, or others.
>
> But since we cannot behold the holiness of God

without worshiping at least no one in the Bible was able
to refrain from worship when God manifested Himself holy
people will want to express themselves in worship. . . . to
God. (*Let Us Be Holy*, Logos International 1978 [Bridge-
Logos Publishers], page 87).

None would declare any person who ever lived as being
more holy than Jesus. Surely His very nature craved for an
opportunity to express itself in worship. Like the sons of Korah,
He cried out, "*As the deer pants for streams of water, so my
soul pants for you, O God. My soul thirsts for God, for the
living God. When can I go and meet with God?,*" and, "*My
soul yearns, even faints, for the courts of the LORD; my heart
and my flesh cry out for the living God*" (Psalm 42:1-2; 84:2).
Worship was far more than a duty to Jesus; it was a necessity.
His Spirit demanded it and His soul craved it.

Jesus could not find fulfillment in worshiping nature, for
He had participated in the creation of everything. He wouldn't
worship persons, even the most religious of His day, for He,
far better than we, knew how seriously sin had deformed
persons from bearing the image of God. He wouldn't worship
Himself even though He knew He was God, for self-worship
is dangerously egocentric and completely unfulfilling. If this
holy servant was to find satisfaction in releasing His holiness
in worship, He had to worship Almighty God and He did this
gloriously.

Jesus, a Worshiper of God

Of course, Jesus worshiped God with His lifestyle. His
actions were expressions of devotion to Father God. However,
there were times when He needed to put into words His inner
feelings and attitudes. Jesus spent long nights in prayer in the
open air, in gardens, and along the seashore; far from the Temple
or synagogues. Surely Jesus' prayer times were more than

seasons of preparing His teachings, speeches, and responses for the day, as we in the preaching ministry are so prone to do. These were not seasons of learning; they were seasons of yearning for an intimate fellowship with His Father.

Jesus was not petitioning the Father in these long prayer sessions. His will was so harmonious with the will of God that pleading with God to do something specific was unnecessary. These were times of fellowship, communion, and communication. Jesus missed the closeness He had enjoyed with His Father, and He made frequent "long distance calls" to Him.

The topic of their communication was far less important than the fact that they just communicated with each other. They were not exchanging facts; they were expressing love. Hear Jesus saying, "*I love you, O LORD, my strength. The LORD is my rock, my fortress and my deliverer; my God is my rock, in whom I take refuge. He is my shield and the horn of my salvation, my stronghold. I call to the LORD, who is worthy of praise*" (Psalm 18:1-3). Other times, He cried out with David, "*The LORD is my strength and my shield; my heart trusts in him, and I am helped. My heart leaps for joy and I will give thanks to him in song*" (Psalm 28:7).

These were times of worship, adoration, and declarations of faith as when He said, "*O LORD, truly I am your servant; I am your servant, the son of your maidservant ; you have freed me from my chains. I will sacrifice a thank offering to you and call on the name of the LORD*" (Psalm 116:16-17). Worship and petition are usually quite distanced from one another. Worship seldom asks, but it frequently gives. Petition is concerned with needs, often very selfish, while worship must, by its very nature, be involved with the person of God.

For Jesus, outer worship rituals were replaced with inner realities. The direction of worship came from the indwelling Spirit rather than from the written words of the Law. Sighing gave way to singing, and sorrow was replaced with joy, for

Jesus had a living object for His worship. The Father was in Him.

None of us is Jesus, yet all born-again believers have Christ living within them. The Apostle John assures us, *"God is love. Whoever lives in love lives in God, and God in him"* and then goes on to say, *"in this world we are like him"* (1 John 4:16-17). This gives us the option to worship God very much as Jesus worshiped Him. Of course we will have our jubilant times of celebrating worship. There will be times of feasting and fasting, singing and shouting with dancing and demonstration, but there will also be times of inner meditation and gentle worship of the Christ within our lives.

As we mature in our Christian experience, we learn that the constancy of our relationship with God is far superior to our times of emotional ecstasy. We discover that our covenant relationship with the Father makes His presence available to us day and night. We find that we need not *"ascend to the hill of God"* to worship, for God has condescended to make His abode in our lives by means of the Holy Spirit. We learn through practical experience what C. Austin Miles meant when he wrote:

> *And He walks with me,*
>
> *And He talks with me,*
>
> *And He tells me I am His own;*
>
> *And the joy we share as we tarry there,*
>
> *None other has ever known.*

(In The Garden, Copyright renewal 1940, The Rodeheaver Co.)

If we will learn to practice our awareness of Christ in us, we will discover that the presence of God the Father, God the Son, and God the Holy Spirit is in us far more than it is among us. God has chosen to live in persons, not dwell in holy places.

He is involved with our lives more than with religious liturgy. In the Old Testament, He revealed Himself to be *Jehovah Shammah*, "I am there." In the New Testament He declares, *"Christ in you, the hope of glory"* (Colossians 1:27). God has consistently sought an intimate relationship with His people. Because of His great love for us, He does not force Himself upon us. It is always the invitation *"Come to me"* (Matthew 11:28).

Jesus the Creator became the creature in order to bring the creation into harmonious fellowship with God. This He has done, is doing, and will continue to do throughout all eternity. He taught us how to worship by the demonstration of His life. He taught us Who to worship by consistently directing His worship to the Father. He taught us where to worship by demonstrating that anywhere He happened to be was a place for worship since God was in Him. He also showed us when to worship by worshiping at all times. He lived in a worship mode. In every way Jesus was a living example of worship!

Now we, who are servants of God, sons of men, and sons of God, can *"Ascribe to the LORD the glory due his name; worship the LORD in the splendor of his holiness"* (Psalms 29:2).